Two Guys Read Moby Dick

T0206644

Steve Chandler & Terrence N. Hill

Robert D. Reed Publishers • Bandon, OR

Robert D. Reed Publishers
P.O. Box 1992
Bandon, OR 97411
Phone: 541-347-9882 • Fax: -9883
E-mail: 4bobreed@msn.com
web site: www.rdrpublishers.com

Typesetter: **Barbara Kruger**
Cover Designer: **Grant Prescott**

ISBN 1-931741-63-8

Library of Congress Control Number 2005930317

Manufactured, typeset and printed in the United States of America

To Miranda

&

To Kathy

Introduction

This didn't start out to be a book. That idea sort of came to us about a third of the way through the correspondence as we got, perhaps unduly, carried away with the brilliance of our insights. Still, even then we were not so deluded as to think that this had John Grisham- or Tom Clancy-like mass-market appeal. No, it would be a quirky book, one with a small select audience.

The potential reader, we felt, would probably meet two essential criteria: 1) the person would have heard of *Moby Dick*, and 2) he or she would probably have some fairly deep emotional attachment to one of the two correspondents. I was able to count five, possibly six, people of my acquaintance that met this standard. Steve, who has a larger family, said he knew at least ten. So we were off and running.

But to back up a bit, this whole thing started late last year when Steve mentioned in an e-mail that he had been at a party where someone had said that the best book he had ever read was *Moby Dick*. On the strength of that recommendation, Steve was planning to read the book.

I wrote back that I would read it with him. And we could encourage and keep tabs on each other's progress by e-mail updates and general commentary on the book. Steve loved the idea and agreed to the project. We started in February of this year. The general plan was to read the book at a rate of ten chapters every two weeks and write our impressions as we went. If you think of the novel as the play-by-play, we saw ourselves as color commentators with a mandate to wander pretty much wherever we wanted when it came to subject matter.

There was never any intention that this be serious literary criticism. It couldn't have been even if we had intended it. For though we are both reasonably well read, we are amateurs. We had no interest in faking it. No part of the "text" would be "deconstructed." And not a single element of the novel would "resonate" with anything. We were just two guys reading *Moby Dick*.

This last happy phrase we felt more or less summed up what this project was all about and consequently became the title of the book you're holding. I believe it was Steve that first hit upon this title, but like many aspects of our friendship, origins and authorship credits get muddy. I once used, off and on for twenty years, a joke of Steve's devising – mentally giving him credit each time I used it, of course, but only mentally. At some point I mentioned to Steve that I had blatantly appropriated his joke for the better part of two decades. He told me that I was quite mistaken and that he was sure the joke was mine rather than his. That kind of thing tends to happen in a long-term friendship. Ours certainly qualifies.

At some moment in September of 2005, Steve and I will have been friends for fifty years. Ike was still in his first term as President when we met in Miss Bonadio's 6th grade class at Adams School in Birmingham, Michigan, initially drawn together by his *Stanley Woodward's College Football Magazine* and a mutual interest in sports. During only about nine of the next fifty years did we live in the same town together, but through visits, phone calls, post cards, letters, and now e-mail, we have always remained close friends and in contact with each other.

Having both been writers all of our working lives, the proposed *Moby Dick* correspondence appealed to us as a project. But in many ways this book is merely the extension of a conversation Steve and I have been having for five decades. Although we recognize this is unlikely, we hope you enjoy it as much as we did.

Terry Hill
15 November 2004 – New York

29 January 2004 – New York

Steve,

I shall start this project off with a confession. You've perhaps heard of that self-embarrassing game that supposedly (or supposed) intellectuals play called "What I Haven't Read." (I heard about the game when it was played by characters in a novel I was reading about academia.) Basically you go around the room and everyone has to name the book they are most embarrassed about not having read.

I called the game self-embarrassing, but when you give it a moment's thought, it's clear that it's actually smugly self-congratulatory, don't you think? It sort of says: I live in a milieu that's so intellectually stringent that not having read *Remembrance of Things Past* or *Gravity's Rainbow* is a source of embarrassment to me.

Anyway, until about three years ago, my book would have been *Ulysses*. But then, in our last year living in Paris, I managed to fight my way through it. I'm not sure what my book would be now, but what it should be (and should have been even before I read *Ulysses*) is *Moby Dick*. The reason it isn't (or hasn't been until now) is that I've always claimed that I *have* read it. In fact I did read about a third of it when it was assigned to us in high school. But I fell behind in the assignment I suppose and then we had the test or I wrote the required paper on it and I simply must not have found the first 180 pages compelling enough to finish it after the classroom need was gone. I already knew the ending after all, having seen the John Huston movie starring Gregory Peck.

So there. That's a load off my conscience: I've never read *Moby Dick*. I look forward to doing my penance in this my sixtieth year. But that raises a question. Since you started this whole thing by suggesting the project last year, have *you* read it? You were in the same year in the same high school as I so you must have also been assigned it. What happened? Or are you just embarking on this as a refresher course? Or perhaps you're in training for a hoped-for slot on "Jeopardy"?

At the launch of this adventure (you'll note how I've gone with your suggestion that nautically-flavored words be employed as much as possible: e.g. "launch" and "embarked") I think it important that you manage your expectations. While I certainly expect you to be a valuable member of this duet, it must be clear that, to the extent a star emerges from this, it would obviously be me. Clearly I am far better suited, by personal geography and inclination, to providing insight and perspective on the book.

In the first place, I live in New York, an historic seaport and a town that still celebrates Fleet Week every year. I might add that 26th Street is also named Herman Melville Street. (I'm not sure why; I suspect he lived there at some point. Before this is over, I'll check into it and let you know the reason.) The point is that just walking these mean streets, as I do everyday, I soak up the salt air and the spirit of Melville. You, on the other hand … well, when was Phoenix's last Fleet Week?

In the second place, there is the undeniable fact that I gave my first born son, as his middle name, the name of the first mate of the Pequod – Starbuck. True. Well, I admit it's also true that I did it because I liked the name and not out of unbound admiration for the work it came from. That's perhaps obvious from my earlier confession that I never finished it; however, that middle name is now in the Hill family Bible.

The third, and clinching argument for my superiority as a *Moby Dick* color man, is the fact that I have, after all, already read the first 180 pages of the book. And that chunk of literature has been boiling away for more than forty years. What a rich broth awaits you, Steve.

I'm hoisting sail right now, and the next you hear from me will be a no doubt trenchant analysis of the book's opening.

Terry.

1 February 2004 – Phoenix

Terry,

Are you really asking if I read the book? You must remember me in high school. Did I read *Pitcairn's Island*?!? Did I have to? No. Not to get my "C" on my book report! Did I even open it? No.

[In our sophomore year for Steve's English mid-term exam, he had to submit, from a list of eligible books, the names of five books he had read in the first half year. For the exam, the teacher would ask an essay question about one of the five books. The problem was you didn't know which book the question would be on. Obviously each student was asked a different question. Steve submitted a list of five books, several of which he may actually have read, though I wouldn't bet on it. Steve's question was on the third book of the Nordoff & Hall Mutiny on the Bounty *trilogy – Pitcairn's Island. Unfortunately he had not read it. Fortunately, neither had his teacher. Steve was asked to describe the native inhabitants of the island. In his answer he wrote in great detail about the strange practices of the natives. Of course, in the book, the island had no natives. He was also asked how the island got its name, giving Steve further opportunity to exercise his imagination. TNH]*

I remember you howling at reading my book report for *Pitcairn's Island* talking about how it got its name from an ancient cave-dwelling mariner, Dr. Pitcairn, and you were laughing so loud I had to snatch it back from you because you would have spoiled my academic strategy by calling attention to the fraud.

Moby Dick was the same. I took a good guess at what it was about and went from there. In college humanities I remember I did a kind of Cliff's Notes rapid scan of it so I could get an "A" on my Humanities final thanks to a huge dose of amphetamines given to the whole house by a fraternity brother doctor.

Now before you get carried away trumpeting your geographical superiority in being able to comment on *Moby Dick*, let me ask you the name of your airport? Ours is called SKY HARBOR. Phoenix Sky Harbor. So don't count your fish before they're hatched.

And finally, GIVE me my deadlines for color commentary. I will follow them religiously. Did you say 20 chapters for the end of February? Give me my precise deadlines…that will help me and will insure that I don't pull a *Pitcairn's Island* on you.

Love to Senorita Miranda.

[Miranda is my wife whose name will naturally appear in these pages a number of times. Steve's wife is Kathy and now's a good time to mention this because her name is also bound to crop up. TNH]

Steve

2 February 2004 – San Miguel de Allende, Guanajuato, Mexico

Steve,

No, I had scheduled only the first ten chapters for February. Are you up to it? Remember it's a short month.

Terry.

2 February 2004

Terry,

Ten chapters by Leap Day? SNAP, dude, but OMIGOD! I'm on chapter 10 right now this guy cannot *write*! He is awkward and in most places godawful!!! Why can't we read Jane Austen? *Two Guys Read Jane Austen!* Because she could write. I mean that girl could write so the STORY (which Melville IS great at spinning, granted!) is a bonus and the WRITING is the great thing, or are the stories in Jane Austen godawful chick stuff?

Steve.

3 February 2004 – San Miguel de Allende, Guanajuato, Mexico

steve,

I brought my *Moby Dick* down here to San Miguel, where we'll be for a month, thinking I'd start this project in a neutral location here in the mountains. You may remember that in 1973 I was in Mexico (Mazatlan) with you, Fred and three now-departed-from-our-lives women. And that on our third day there I got very sick. Very sick. Well, the same thing happened here.

So there I was lying on the couch yesterday in our apartment here, knowing that I would not be going anywhere that day and vaguely thinking how pleasant death might be. I decided this might be a good day to start the book. I wasn't exactly full of ambition, but I did set as a modest goal, Melville's two preface sections: "Etymology" and "Extracts."

I loved his tribute to the "sub-sub-librarian" who putatively gathered all those whale and whaling quotes for him. I counted about sixty quotes there. It must have been a big job for someone to have collected all those whale extracts back in those days.

Imagine how easy it would have been if the sub-sub-librarian (who was obviously really Melville himself) had had the services of Google.

But now I have a question: what was Melville's point in giving us that packet of miscellany up front? Everything from biblical spoutings and Shakespeare to gory first person accounts of whale hunts to sea songs. What was he trying to do? Is it all just sort of meant to establish the novel's territory?

Last night as I was drifting toward a feverish sleep I was thinking about some of these extracts. This was a mistake. I always have nightmares when I'm running a fever and this night I lived in a Melville-induced bad acid trip. Whales were ramming my flimsy boat and throwing me into the frenzied waters; blood was gushing in gallons; and blubber was being violently hacked. It was not a fun night. But by the morning, the calm had returned. I was feeling markedly better and the Melville phantasmagoria had receded back to within the covers of the book. But you see, Steve, once again I have one-upped you. For while you are merely reading *Moby Dick*, I have lived it.

Let me go back to a thought that occurred to me when I mentioned our Mazatlan trip in '73. Why is it the three women who were on that trip with us are now gone from our lives? We, on the other hand, have been not only in contact with each other, but friends before and since. Was it just the coincidence of these three particular women? It's not as if they were just casual acquaintances; two of them after all were actually married to us. I suspect it has more to do with what women expect of men, what they want of us. In the end, they get impatient and leave us (or cause us to leave them, which is the same thing really) because, of course, we are unable to live up to their expectations and desires. The root of this failure, I believe, lies in our status as mortal beings.

Men, on the other hand, take other men pretty much as they find them. We don't see other men as potentially perfectible projects. We don't construct fairy tale castles out of them. I mean how perfect does a guy have to be for me to get some enjoyment out of watching a ball game with him? Or to have a couple of beers and a little low-level conversation with?

What is it in women that they cannot see us the way we are? To quote the famous gender philosopher Rex Harrison, "Why can't a woman be more like a man?"

Terry.

15 February 2004 – Phoenix

Dear Pickering,

I was just talking about Rex Harrison to a friend yesterday.

Sorry about your illness…reminds me of Juarez when your best friend the doctor wouldn't even tell you what you'd got. Or was that Dylan's doctor?

I actually have the highest standards in history for a male close friend, which is why you are my friend. Sure, I can watch a game with some flawed loser of a male buddy, but I can't stay with him for years and delight in his every communication.

I've read my 10 chapters and will comment soon.

Meanwhile, defensive stats for Jeter and A-Rod for the last five years from ESPN:

Jeter

Year	Errors	Fielding%	Range factor	Games
2003	14	.969	3.75	118
2002	14	.977	3.81	156
2001	15	.974	3.81	150
2000	24	.961	4.12	148
1999	14	.978	4.00	158

A-Rod

Year	Errors	Fielding%	Range factor	Games
2003	8	.989	4.54	158
2002	10	.987	4.73	162
2001	18	.976	4.72	161
2000	10	.986	4.76	148
1999	14	.977	4.82	129

So, A-Rod averages about a 0.75 better range factor and consistently has a better fielding percentage as well. That means he gets to more balls, makes more plays and commits fewer errors per chance. Unless you have some esoteric reason for thinking Jeter is a better fielder, like "he makes the big plays" or "he does it in the NY spotlight" or some other rationale that can't be backed up by facts, then you have to admit the obvious.

Love to Senora M.

s.

15 February 2004 – San Miguel de Allende

Dear Bill James,

[In editing this correspondence, both my wife and Steve's queried the name Bill James so I suppose it needs an explanation. In baseball circles, James is famous for being the man who brought rigorous mathematical analysis to the sport. TNH]

Here we are in search of the big fish and you seem intent on distracting me with miscellaneous baseball numbers. Is this a follow-up to some discussion on Derek vs. A-Rod that you think you had with me at some point? If so, let me set the record straight:

As much as I love Jeter, and as good as I think he is, I have *always* maintained that the position is so strong right now that he is right now only the third best shortstop in the American League even. (Garciaparra being the other ahead of him).

But I also maintain that Jeter and the Yankees will again win a pennant while A-Rod and the Rangers will again finish last.

t.

15 February 2004 – Phoenix

terry.

A-Rod IS a Yankee!! Don't you get the news down there in Mexico?

s.

15 February 2004 – San Miguel de Allende

steve.

We get only one English language paper here and we missed getting it yesterday. What happened?!? Who'd they have to give up to get him? Never mind, I'll check cnnsi.com for details right now. Thanks for keeping me up to date.

t.

16 February 2004 – San Miguel de Allende

Steve,

I swear to you this is the truth. And the truth shall set us free from any lingering doubt whether we're reading the right book.

On Valentine's Day I took Miranda to a classy restaurant here called the Sierra Nevada en la Parque. We were a little early so we went to the bar for a drink first. The waiter in the bar was dressed in a white smock top with one of those black candy-bar-size plastic nameplates with reversed white letters on his chest. His name was Ishmael. I mean it could be a coincidence, but then I thought about it: have you ever, at any time during your fifty-nine-plus years on earth, run into anyone named Ishmael?

This is no coincidence; hell, this is portent.

Naturally I couldn't quietly note this sign and just let it go. This was there to be used. So when I wanted a drink, I asked Miranda to: "Call me Ishmael." She is kind enough to be fairly tolerant of these little word plays, which are the addiction of the former copywriter, but I know this kind of thing wears thin on normal human beings. And even I have questioned the wisdom of letting it go unchecked.

So I came to a resolution. I will not turn this correspondence into a pun-fest. I shall stay away from nautical or whaling word plays for the duration. Well, no sooner had I steeled myself to resist temptation than I was reading chapter 2. And right there as Melville, or perhaps more properly Ishmael, is describing the Spouter Inn he goes off on a tangent.

He starts crying the blues about... Well, to be honest, who knows what it's about? As near as I can figure out (and I refuse to read it a *fourth* time) he's wailing away about some big wind or storm called Euroclydon. And Lazarus. And God tell me what else. All of a sudden he pulls himself up short and says: "But no more of this blubbering now, we are going a-whaling, and there is plenty of that yet to come."

Well right away my zero-tolerance for word play resolve is shaken. I mean if Melville himself can dance the jig then who am I to sit this one out? So now I amend my unshakable resolution. From now on I have decided I shall allow word play if it happens accidentally or subconsciously. I will not edit it out, but I will not go in search of it. So now I feel semi-virtuous. Even though I allow my little *jeu d'mots*, I can still feel superior to Melville because "blubbering" was no accident.

On your nagging doubts about the quality of Melville's writing ("Cannot *write*," was the phrase you used I believe.), I would urge patience. I have found that reading writers from past eras it sometimes takes a bit of time before you start catching the clicks of their conventions, before you fall into the rhythms of their styles.

You mentioned Jane Austen a few days ago. I've read all six of her novels, several of them twice, and one of them (P&P) four times. Obviously I'm a fan. And yet every time I start one I find the first twenty or thirty pages pretty sticky and suddenly some switch is thrown and it goes smoothly for me the rest of the way.

I say all this in a spirit of hope because I can't really say that the opening ten chapters have led me to believe that this is going to be my all time favorite novel either. The effect the mannered and slightly fussy style had on me was that – since the novel is told in the first person – it made me think of Ishmael as a bit pretentious. But maybe, I thought, we were meant to feel this. Maybe Melville was setting him up for a bit of humbling when the whaling began.

For instance, consider that other contender for the title "The Great American Novel," *Huckleberry Finn*. It is also told in the first person, but you never mistake that voice for anyone's but Huck's. In *Moby Dick* we tend to think of the mannered style as being Melville's, and perhaps it is, but it could also be Melville creating the character of Ishmael.

Once again, this is written in hope because … well, I started this whole thing with a confession, perhaps it's time for another:

I am one of those guys who finishes every book he starts. That's not quite true as you'll see, but pretty darn close. You are going to tell me this is stupid, but I already know that. It's merely an illness that I have accepted and have learned to live with. Yes, of course it's stupid to get fifty or a hundred pages into a four hundred page book, realize you hate it and have no interest in it, and then spend another ten hours or so fighting your way through the rest of it. And yet, as often as this has happened to me in my life, I can count on the fingers of one hand (okay, the fingers *plus* the thumb) the books I have begun and not finished. One of these is *Moby Dick*, as you already know. But the further bad news is that another of the five is *The Confidence Man* – also by Melville. In fact, the only Melville book I've ever been able to finish is *Billy Budd* and that's not even long enough to be called a novel.

On the positive side though, let me say that I like the way the novel has an easy-paced walking start. I know that's not very popular now and that the vogue is for novels to start "*in medias res*" in emulation of so many films. But I like to amble into a plot. I want to know the territory we're in and get to know the lead character a bit before anything more exciting than trying to find a cheap hotel room for the night starts to happen.

I'll also say that by the time Ishmael starts building a friendship with Queequeg I'm starting to warm up to both Ishmael and the style. As the song says, I'm in full sail right now.

Two last things:

Coming into this project I thought of the Gregory Peck version of *Moby Dick*. I know I saw the film (very likely, by the way, with you), but the only thing I actually remembered about the film was the climactic scene of Ahab with the whale. However, while I was reading Ishmael's meeting with Queequeg at the Spouter Inn section, that scene from the movie came back to me vividly.

That's quite an accomplishment for a film, I think, to impress a scene on your mind so deeply that with a little prompt, the film starts running in your mind again over forty years later. I wonder who played Queequeg?

Another thing, quite unrelated, was an association that came to me in chapter 1. It's the section where Ishmael is talking about how he doesn't really mind taking orders from ship's officers and being made to polish brass and swab decks. "Who ain't a slave?" he says philosophically. The Bob Dylan song "You've Got To Serve Someone" immediately popped into my mind when I read that because, of course, it's really the same thought.

But since you had earlier mentioned Dylan (in the context of my being dog-sick down here) it struck me exactly how iconic Dylan has become. I mean from being a singer whose next album I always wanted to hear, he has grown to maybe the most quoted man in the country. I have no statistics to support that, but I'll bet I'm not that far off.

So anyway, don't put on any airs when you're down on Rue Morgue Avenue, bye.

t.

18 February 2004 – Phoenix

terry,

I heed your call to patience on *Moby Dick*. I am starting to get used to the style. I will not throw this book across the room as I do so many books that are recommended to me as brilliant and turn out to be shallow, obvious, derivative and stupid. For me, most fiction today falls into that category.

That's the difference between you and me. You finish every book you start while I finish about 20% of the books I start. On the other hand, I read about three books a week. I'm not proud of that because it's obsessive. I read for business reasons to learn new concepts that I can teach in my seminars and I read other books to escape and I read a lot of spiritual books to see a bigger picture of myself and I read a lot of poetry now and of course always Nabokov. I generally have about six books going at once all over the house. I read many books more than once – the ones that really made a difference. I like Isaac Asimov because he wrote more books (800 plus?) than the average person has read.

Your reference to being in "full sail" quotes a very obscure song indeed. It's called "Tall Hope" from an old musical, "Wildcat!" starring Lucille Ball. I only know it (and can play it on my guitar) because it was once part of the repertoire of Elektra Records folk music artist Bob Grossman (fairly obscure himself) whom I used to go watch sing in a Tucson coffee house called Ash Alley.

[I worry about Steve and Alzheimer's. The only reason I quoted that song is because it was Steve that taught it to me sometime in the early '60s. TNH]

I hope *Moby Dick* turns out to be as great as its rep, but right now, that's a "tall hope."

Because you do not embrace metaphysics as I do, I will take this opportunity to educate you. To bring you up to date. The bartender named Ishmael? Full scale synchronicity! When a major synchronicity like that happens, it means God is winking at you. That you are on your path and doing the right thing in life.

In fact, I had a minor synchronicity (compared to yours) with the first part of the book. I had watched, the night before, the Westminster Kennel Championships dog show on TV. And the surprise Best of Show was a huge black Newfoundland dog. It was very exciting to watch, as you can surely imagine. Then, the next morning, the very first page I read contained this description of Queequeg by Melville. "I succeeded in extracting a grunt, and presently, he drew back his arm, and shook himself all over like a Newfoundland dog just from the water."

Wink.

If Dylan is not the number one quoted person in America right now, he's right up there. Dylan and Yogi Berra I'd say, with Emerson a distant third. Although, Winston Churchill is the most often quoted person in the Oxford English Dictionary.

Steve.

24 February 2004 -- Phoenix

Terry.

Moby Dick is a thunderous book, like twisted rebar coming from fragmented concrete its sentences in their stilted, lofty descriptions are not a joy to read for me. They made me understand even more why Hemingway tried to go the opposite direction. "We ate the meal. The meal was good."

Stylistically Hemingway was the anti-Melville, capturing the same manly adventure but with language he had worked and worked into the simplest most straightforward presentation he could make.

(I just looked up this year's winner in the Hemingway Parody contest, it's Brandon Fuller, and here's a sample of his work: "As I was driving down the highway, I saw a lovely bug splatter upon my lovely window. Now this bug is not good, but my bottle of Drano was, so I drank it, and it was good. It had been good for some time now. I took a nice pull of my drink again. It was still good.")

Moby Dick has thunder and cross-thunder in content, too, which is not a gift to me. The bellows from the preacher introduce a Biblical parallel to the story we are about to hear. On the basis of the story of Jonah, Father Mapple tells the worshippers to keep away from the path of evil. According to him, in order to follow God's path, one has to deny one's own temptations and interests.

Yet the sea tempts Ishmael. The sea, to him, is perhaps the source of all life. At the very least when things on land get too testy and morbid, the sea calls.

Is the sea the source of all life? I hear now it's the stars. That we humans are made of stars. That the primary chemical components of our bodies originated in stars. I don't want to buck that star theory nor do I want to let go of the idea that we all come from the sea.

But I do buck the scene when the preacher uses the old mythology of Jonah to roar down on people and their temptations. That is not a gift to me. I like gifts in my reading, which is why I love Nabokov so much. I can (and do) open *Ada* to any portion of the book and read three pages and it is pure poetry, a gift in those three pages. Those pages don't set up or condition me for some future plot twist (they do, actually, but that's just one of the many parallel universes, not the main thing, like in Melville, the linear, pounding, overly-obvious thunderously depth-inserting Melville.)

I don't swim well. Do we come from the sea? When I'm at my best, I do shine at times. That would be a vote for the stars. Terry Hill you are quoted in my first book, the motivational classic *100 Ways to Motivate Yourself,* for the time (which I had on tape) in your Creativity serminar delivered to advertising types when you quoted Salinger's advice to writers to "get your stars out" when you are writing.

I won't buck any of that.

I fear the water, generally. I'm not drawn to it, physically, although I love La Jolla, a walk by the water is fantastic, fighting waves as you and I did in Mazatlan was great because you introduced competition. *Men Against the Sea.* Wasn't that a book in the series that finished with *Pitcairn's Island*? My wife Kathy thinks she went down on the Titanic. She has past life dreams and reacted badly to the DiCaprio movie.

Moby Dick introduces a charming heathen. Is that so ironic that he is a heathen and seems so spiritual? Is that heavy? That the preacher Mapples seems so not spiritual?

I noticed that in Hollywood movies. For years now they've liked to have a black person play a kind of sage and saint. Morgan Freeman has played many of those roles…reparations for the days when blacks were portrayed as frightened fools. You ask me who played Queequeg. I believe it was Morgan Freeman.

In the first 10 chapters of *Moby Dick* we are not yet at sea. We have established first person story teller Ishmael, and his new powerfully subtle heathen pal Queequeg the pagan, cannibalistic heathen.

I must say though, that I haven't found any writing in this book yet. Am I a party pooper for saying that? It's a whale of a tale, as far as stories go thus far, and there's philosophy about the sea and sin and all that profundity that's as clumsy as a piano played with mittens on. But where is the writing? Where is the gift?

I visited a friend this past weekend whom I hadn't seen in 42 years! He was in high school with us, and he gave me a gift. He said "I am reading *Don Quixote*. I am reading it so you don't have to. DON'T read this book! It is ponderous and awful!"

Moby Dick may get better. At any rate, I will keep reading it because I know that not to do so would deprive myself of what you think of it and that, knowing you, will include some writing, and that, knowing you, is where I'll get the gift I'm looking for.

Steve.

2 March 2004 – Back in New York

Steve.

Okay, is this some kind of tease? Who was the not-seen-in-42-years friend who went to high school with us? The only person I can think of from high school who would be likely to be reading

Don Quixote is Roger Mason. Or maybe Tolly Jo Dickson. (You didn't specify whether it was a male or a female friend. And while we're at it, did we really know someone named Tolly Jo?)

Also in your last e-mail you made reference to an advertising creativity seminar I used to give. Except that you wrote "serminar." This is either an out-and-out mistake; a thinly veiled suggestion that my public speeches and seminars were too preachy; or a brilliant neologism denoting a business seminar with a spiritual dimension. It also works nicely with your reference to the Reverend Mapple's fire-and-brimstone sermon. Anyway, after all the praise you piled on me in the last paragraph of that e-mail, I am fully prepared to give you full credit for the creation of a new and useful word.

I am e-mailing it to Noah Webster right now for inclusion in his next edition. (And if you doubt Noah has an e-mail address, let me ask you who is more likely to have a website than "The Web-ster?")

God, this is a long way from Melville, but have you ever read Updike's *A Month of Sundays*? It's about a minister who has trespassed majorly against the church (perhaps against God too, but since there are a whole bunch of issues on which I'm not sure where God stands right now, I'll just wait and see on that). The minister may also be having a mental breakdown as well. So he's stripped of his congregation and banished to a retreat/rest home where he has regular sessions with a psychiatrist who has him keep a daily journal where he works through his problems on paper. Updike's novel is this journal. One of the conceits in the novel is that the minister makes all kinds of spelling errors or malapropisms that, of course, turn out to be Freudian slips and quite wonderful word plays. Your "serminar" reminded me of that.

You know how people are always putting down puns and word plays. The traditional sign of this is the stagy groan or the much exaggerated rolling of eyes. Supposedly this signals the low regard they have for these childish verbal games. But, of course, what they're really trying to do is say: "Look how intellectual and quick I am to have gotten the pun without anybody having to poke me in the ribs." I think it's interesting that as much as this form is held as low art, a number of our finest writers have absolutely reveled in it. I cite Updike, Joyce and Nabokov merely as the first three that come to mind. All of them clearly had the addiction and totally gave themselves up to it.

Yes, I agree that the "irony" of Queequeg, the heathen, being the spiritually and morally superior being is a bit heavy handed. You know who did this thing better – or at least a lot more subtly? Twain in Huck Finn. He's got overly superstitious and underly educated Jim – played, no doubt, by Morgan Freeman – winding up as the moral center of the novel.

I looked up the John Huston/Gregory Peck version of *Moby Dick*, by the way, to find out who did play Queequeg, but it wasn't listed in the book I had. I found a couple of surprises in the credits however. The Reverend Mapples was played by Orson Welles (for whom the word "thundering" was invented). And the screenplay? Ray Bradbury. When we get a bit further in the book, I think I'll rent it and see it again. It came out in 1956, and since I met you in the fall of 1955, it's very likely that I saw it with you.

Back to you.

t.

5 March 2004 -- Phoenix

terry.

"Serminar" was a typographical error guided by the cosmic hand of The Punster, as in The Webster. Or Mel Gibson's The Christ.

Our 42-year-ago high school classmate was Christoph Hoffmann, then German foreign exchange student, now American lawyer. A dear and bright man. He was in Tucson with me for a day when I told him that two guys were reading *Moby Dick* and he remembered you well.

Surprisingly Morgan Freeman did not play Queequeg, at least not in the 1956 John Huston version. I looked it up. It was James Robertson. I really don't think I saw it though – none of it comes back to me. Today I think the Queequeg role would go to Eminem because the tattoos would be just right.

I did like the way Melville had Ishmael rationalize why he was going to pray to Queequeg's idol, thinking that no god of any kind of generosity or charity would mind.

Orson Welles (Huston's Mapples) is no relation to David Wells, the leviathan pitcher formerly of the Yankees whose other coincidental nickname may be whale blubber. Wells was so overfed and porcine last year that he had to take himself out of a World Series game because his fat had pulled some muscles loose and he could not stand up straight.

s.

14 March 2004 – Phoenix

Terry.

As we read the next ten chapters we are not yet sailed to the sea but we are getting some foreshadowing of the mysterious and powerful Captain of this ship – Captain Ahab.

Because you introduced the subject of Bob Dylan, I had to think about Bob Dylan's 115th Dream "…when I thought I spied some land…I yelled for Captain AY-rab…" and wondered about the parallel of the song to *Moby Dick*.

Also because Ishmael and Queequeg are about to set sail and all the trappings of preparing for the voyage are so thoroughly described by Melville I decided to read up a little on Melville's life, out of curiosity. And yes he sailed and whaled throughout his life. He was also a voracious reader who devoured books while not writing them.

I found out that in the summer of 1851, at work on *Moby Dick*, Melville reminisced in a letter to his friend and hero Nathaniel Hawthorne: "Until I was twenty-five, I had no development at all. From my twenty-fifth year I date my life. Three weeks have scarcely passed, at any time between then and now, that I have not unfolded within myself."

Curious to me, although I don't compare myself to Melville as I write my own motivational books, I, like you, have always been some sort of writer, be it country music, advertising copy or motivational books.

And I myself have experienced this kind of unfoldment that Melville describes, and I date mine to the time when I stopped my drinking. And I was so helped by your father Art Hill who began his own unfoldment late in life. I see unfoldment, as Melville describes it, as a creative flowering in the inside of one's brain or mind or soul, whichever term applies. Just this week I read your memorial essay to your father and the commentary on his new writing life after his drinking, and the terrific writing he did right up to the end.

I only bring this up because of the coincidence that overcame me a few nights ago when watching TV (yes I channel surf which is why I can't remember the show as I flew past it) and I heard someone quote from *Moby Dick*! (And here I've worried that we were writing a book about something long ago lost to the culture.) On the TV show someone quoted Ishmael's line after finding out he would have to sleep in the same bed with the pagan Queequeg, "Better to sleep with a sober cannibal than a drunken Christian."

steve

Steve.   15 March 2004

Your mention of my father reminds me that he died sixteen years ago tomorrow. When did you quit drinking, by the way?

When I was about twenty-five I went through a Nathaniel Hawthorne phase. I'm not sure why exactly, but I suspect it had something to do with discipline, a quality I revere but have very little aptitude for. Was I going to do a Sherman's March to the Sea on American literature starting with Hawthorne? (I suppose I should have started with Emerson but I find him almost as impossible to read as Gertrude Stein – in a different way of course.) Whatever the reason for this Hawthorne thing, I don't regret it. I read virtually all of his books. Not just the novels, but also the short stories, the fables and some non-fiction. I even read the Henry James biography of him. I remember really quite liking *Blithedale Romance, The House of Seven Gables* and *The Scarlet Letter*. My favorite part of *The Scarlet Letter* is, however, the customs house section which starts the book rather than the actual tale of Hester itself.

Anyway, this is all to say that I picked up a lot of Trivial-Pursuit type information on Hawthorne at the time. So did you know that Hawthorne wrote the campaign biography for Franklin Pierce? They had been college buddies at Bowdoin. Pierce, by the way, had a serious drinking problem though I doubt Hawthorne mentioned that in the bio. After he was elected, Pierce rewarded Hawthorne by giving him a cushy posting in Europe, out of which came the novel *The Marble Faun* I believe.

It's interesting that Hawthorne and Melville were such chums. Certainly they had totally different lives and wrote very different kinds of books. Melville, as you point out, had spent a good bit of time at sea, whereas Hawthorne led sort of a cloistered, bookish life. Obviously, however, they were close and we have Melville's dedication of *Moby Dick* to Hawthorne as evidence. That always used to be one of my favorite literary trivia questions, which of course I can't stump you with now. I can try another one, however. A three parter:

    1) Who is *The Waste Land* dedicated to?

    2) Who was the best man at William Butler Yeats wedding?

    3) Who was William Carlos Williams' best friend when he was in medical school at the University of Pennsylvania?

How can you even suggest that *Moby Dick* has lost its importance in American culture? Not only do you have the proof of the quote you heard on television and Bob Dylan (Which album is the "115th Dream" on, anyway?), but also there is a show that just opened on Broadway based on *Moby Dick*. Sounds awful doesn't it?

Also I think the book survives for Americans, and especially American writers as "the one to beat." It's almost axiomatic that if you're going to write the "great American novel," you gotta beat *Moby Dick*.

Have you ever read Philip Roth's book *The Great American Novel*? It's about baseball, not whaling, but the book is dotted with references to *Moby Dick*. And I read an interview with Roth on the book in which he pretty much acknowledged my "one to beat" point. He also said that, for America, he saw baseball as the 20th century's myth-making factory in the same way that whaling served that function for Melville in the 19th century.

This, of course, raises the obvious question: if Ishmael and Queequeg (aka Quohog) were in a 20th century novel, what positions would they play? Ishmael is easy. I see him as a born second baseman. Queequeg is harder. He's either a fleet-footed right fielder who bats third in the order, or he's a starting pitcher. The French word for pitcher (as you would know if you'd ever seen the Expos play in Montreal) is *le lanceur*, which seems to me pretty close to harpooner. Am I wrong?

I must say that I'm starting to like Ishmael. In these last ten chapters he seems no longer pretentious and even kind of funny now and then. Witness the scene with his landlady when he's desperate to break down the door to get in his room when he thinks that Queequeg is in distress. Or his comment that "hell is an idea first born on an undigested apple-dumpling."

Or his assessment that Queequeg "cherished Yojo with considerable esteem as a rather good sort of god, who perhaps meant well enough upon the whole, but in all cases did not succeed in his benevolent designs."

Come to think of it, this last is pretty much how I see our God – the one with the capitalized G.

As you can tell from the date at the top of this letter I was going to send this last night (the 15th). We went out to dinner, however, and when we got back it was late and I was tired, so I missed my deadline. The good part is that this tardiness on my part means that I was able to see in this morning's *New York Times* a rave review of the play *Moby Dick* that I mentioned earlier – "luminous and engrossing." The whole thing is done in an hour and a quarter. I'll send the review on to you by regular mail.

t.

17 March 2004

terry.

Yes, *Moby Dick* as a musical does sound awful. It reminds me of a place I used to drink at. It was in a Polynesian restaurant and they had women swimming in a huge fish tank behind the bar. I quit drinking twenty-four years ago and haven't been back since. I believe you *had* to be drinking to go to that place. That's what the idea of this *Moby Dick* play reminds me of.

I can imagine the play having a great rhythm and blues song for Queequeg, "I Got My Yojo Workin'."

I also loved that hell/undigested-apple-dumpling quote, and it's my idea of hell too, not unlike Thomas Szasz's conclusion that "all concepts of a literal hell are a form of mental illness." Or fatigue. Same thing.

You are right about Ishmael. He is the truth-telling rascal Melville adores and wants his reader to be charmed by because of his buddy-movie bonding with Queequeg and his ability to lance the cartoon follies of myth-bound religions.

I suspect you are also right about Ishmael's rightful position being second base. The thing that bothers me a bit is that we've read 20 chapters so far and I still can't anticipate how he will get the nickname "Rocket."

As to Queequeg's baseball position, I see him as a closer. A hoser of a harpooning closer, maybe from Canada like the Dodger's closer is, like the mad Hungarian type closers who are hosers and intimidate batters with their wild ways on the mound, harpooning the ball in there in that final inning. They just reach back and whale.

And finally. "The Waste Land" dedicatee? Yeats's best man? W.C. Williams pal? I want to say George Plimpton for all these, and I think I'm right. So, yes, I'm going with George Plimpton. Man of letters George. *Paris Review* George. Lion George. Though paper.

s.

30 March 2004 – NYC.

Steve.

> Pound. Pound. Pound.
> Ezra's the answer –
> for all three.
> Not George Plimpton,
> though that was a damn fine guess.
> It was Pound.
> Pound. Pound. Pound.
> Amazing, isn't it?

Can you tell from the character of that first paragraph that I've just been reading poetry? Yes, Jim Harrison in a wonderful little book called Braided Creek (which I'm sending on to you) and then Billy Collins, who despite being Poet Laureate of these United States during a Republican administration (2001-2003) seems slight to me in comparison with Harrison.

Anyway, have you heard it said that *Moby Dick* is poetry? I've read that several times by people who should know better. Sometimes they hedge their bet by saying *parts* of it are poetry. Honestly, I've read that. I can't see it myself.

Early on you characterized the writing as thunderous. I would call it clanging. It seems to move like an old steam engine, clanging. I don't find it unpleasant, in fact it has a certain charm, but I sure don't find it the stuff of poetry. The style – like the book – feels sturdy and utilitarian to me and nowhere more so than in these last ten chapters. It's as if Melville is laying the foundation here brick by brick: Ahab is set up as a troubled, and troubling, mystery. Then we have the two identically named chapters ("Knights and Squires") in which each of the mates and their harpooners are set up. Then we have those two chapters which are merely arguments for the importance of whaling. What are those all about? They would seem more appropriate in a treatise on 19th century economics. You get the sense that Melville did a lot of research and was bound and determined to use what he's picked up somewhere – so he just stuck it in here.

And yet despite all the foresaid, I'm actually enjoying it. This big, clunky, clanging novel, written before authors aspired to read the phrase "elegant novel" in reviews of their books. No, this is the book for which the term "sprawling novel" was invented.

One thing that struck me is that maybe the unnatural way we are reading the novel is coloring our reactions to it. I'm not sure exactly how, but it seems a possibility. Am I seeing the book as something to slog through because of the slow pace I'm reading it? I don't actually think so, but maybe. Ordinarily I get into a book and move along at a pretty steady comfortable pace until at some point the book clicks in for me and then my pace very much accelerates and I fly through the rest of the book. Here, I'm reading the allotted chapters slowly by the due date, then thinking about them, then skimming the chapters again desperately trying to find something half way interesting to say or comment on before I actually write you. I feel like I'm reining myself in all the time. Not allowing the book to take the bit between its teeth – denying it the "click" and the acceleration.

I'm actually enjoying the discipline of the whole process, but I wonder if it affects our perception of the book. You think?

My text for today comes from the first paragraph of chapter 27. In speaking of Stubb, Melville writes: "What he thought of death itself, there is no telling. He took it to be … something he would find out about when he obeyed the order, and not sooner."

I suppose it's pretty well understood nowadays that we are all required to think about death. Not just to think about it, but to "contemplate" it. It is the mark of the philosophically aware man, is it not?

My question is: what's the point? What does it gain us to contemplate death? Estate planners tell us that the reason for the contemplation of death is that we not leave a chaotic mess for people we love to clean up after we've caught the Red-Eye. And I can certainly go along with that. But that's not contemplation, that's really only the acknowledgment of the inevitability of death.

I'm asking what is the point of the mournful staring-at-the-sea (or desert in your case) while sitting in an Adirondack chair and just ... contemplating ... death?

Having raised that question, I must admit I'm as guilty as anyone of indulging in this. There was a time in my mid-thirties when the concept of death first hit me and it haunted me for several years. This has to be an almost universal experience I suspect. I really wondered at the meaning of life. Eventually I concluded that it had *no* meaning. Now many people would think this a disillusioning and depressing conclusion.

I found it liberating. And I believe I've lived a much more purposeful life since, though I do this in a fairly desultory way, I admit. My sense is that if there is no "official" meaning of life, then it becomes my responsibility to come up with one and live up to it, doesn't it? This is the ultimate self-help discipline, the ultimate taking responsibility for one's own life. Not only do you take responsibility for its conduct, you also take responsibility for its meaning.

Anyway, once I sorted all that out in my head, I really never gave death much thought for the next twenty years or so. Lately, however, it's grabbed a hold of me again. I don't think a day goes by now that I don't think about death at some point. It's different now though. I don't think of it with the terror I did in my thirties, but rather as a well-meaning, but still annoyingly nagging friend who keeps reminding me of all the things I haven't done and pushes me to get on the stick.

Death as the ultimate personal trainer.

Sail on, Mr. Stubb, toward that final destination to which you have given no thought and over which you have no control.

I felt it necessary to put in these profound thoughts on death because of something someone once said to me about Saul Bellow. She said that Bellow would not have won the Nobel Prize unless he had written *Humbolt's Gift*. (He was awarded the Prize soon after he came out with *Gift*.) Because, she suggested, you cannot win the Prize without tackling the "big themes."

Humbolt's Gift is about death. (College Board question: A novel that starts with a funeral and ends with a funeral is about _____. Fill in the blank.) And while you can argue about what the "big themes" are, death is pretty much odds-on to make everybody's list. Anyway, if this correspondence is going to be a book, I certainly didn't want us to be ruled off the Nobel Prize short-list just because we failed to deal with death.

And finally. Miranda watched "Star Trek: First Contact" on television last night and told me the film makes allusion to, and even quotes, *Moby Dick* several times. We're where it's at.

t.

March 31, 2004

RE: MDICK (*not marilyn but moby)

[The asterisked note is a reference to a girl we both knew in high school – a bright girl of iconic WASP suburban good looks named Marilyn Dick. TNH]

t.

In these chapters Melville is introducing us to the people on the ship. Starbuck is the one I want to be. Remember when we were kids and we wanted to BE certain characters? I want to be Starbuck. Maybe Melville wants to be Starbuck, too? I don't know yet......but I do. Why?

Because his flesh is as "hard as twice-baked biscuit."

And mine is not. Because the first venture in this "two guys" series (Two Guys Lose Weight) was not pursued long or seriously enough by me and I ballooned up again! How humiliating to be an actual PART of America's obesity problem. Whale-like in appearance, I became totally ashamed. So I am in earnest now, and I want my flesh to be hard, not soft. I want to be hard like Starbuck, hard as twice-baked biscuit.

So I've lost three pounds in my journey back to my high school weight.

[The year before this correspondence began, Steve and I, both feeling a bit overweight began diets at the same time. As with the reading of Moby Dick, we sent e-mails back and forth talking about the dieting experience. We pretty much followed the standard diet pattern, showing early success and then fervor for the discipline. I think I may have eventually reached my target weight. Steve didn't. TNH]

Another thing about Starbuck as Melville describes him to us is his courage, or rather, his access to his courage. I love it. "Starbuck was no crusader after perils" but rather someone who had courage available to him whenever he needed it.

I so love that in the man and aspire to it. Is it too late in life to be Starbuck? To go after one's own whale? Never. In fact, this is a near-obsession with me. When I successfully utilized the 12-step program to recover from alcoholism I noticed that the "Serenity Prayer" was read at the beginning of every meeting: "God grant me the serenity to accept the things I cannot change, the courage to change the things I can, and the wisdom to know the difference."

Everyone calls it "the serenity prayer." Everyone except me. I call it "The Courage Prayer." Grant me the courage to change the things I can. Such as my weight. Such as the fact that I have never read *Moby Dick*.

What I like about Melville's description, short foreshadowing character-sketch of Starbuck the Chief Mate, is his revelation that he believes all men have courage deep down. This is something I believe, too. We all have the same infinite well of courage. It isn't whether we "have" it it's whether we use it. We all have an arm. Who uses his most has the strongest.

Steve.

15 April 2004 – New York

Steve.

In my last letter I mentioned the concept of death as the ultimate reminder to get something done today. I had that idea a few years ago but I think that letter was the first time I had ever put it into words. Last night Miranda and I went to a play called "Hannah and Martin." The play follows the fascinating relationship between Hannah Arendt and Martin Heidegger. Hannah was a Jewish student in Germany when at 18, and twenty years his junior, she has an affair with him. Nine years later he became a member of the Nazi Party and Hitler's showcase intellectual. Perhaps his only intellectual.

Anyway, in the course of the play, Heidegger, played by David Strathairn (Do you know him? A terrific actor I think.), at various times expounds his ideas. One of them was pretty much a paraphrase of my death-as-deadline idea. The point is that no matter how many years ago I had the idea, it's pretty certain that Heidegger had it first.

This seems to happen to me a lot. I'm sure it's a pretty common experience for everyone. You have an idea which you think is your own and then later you discover the idea has been in circulation for some time.

I have a mixed reaction whenever this happens. At first I am rather chuffed that Heidegger (or Einstein or Bellow or whoever) had the same I idea I had. It seems a sort of validation. But then the whole thing starts gnawing at me – it begins to seem as if I've never had an original thought in my life, which is, of course, rather discouraging. But should it be? I've heard it said many times before that there are no new ideas. Just modifications, revivals, rearrangements and new combinations of old ideas. I can live with that I guess.

Don't you find these last ten chapters (31 through 40) a strange mix? I started out on this trip with the strong expectation that this would be an epic story – much like the *Iliad* or the *Odyssey* (another sea voyage story). You made a similar comment early on when you acknowledged the "yarn" aspect of the book.

But by chapter 41 I'm getting a very different impression. This is hardly the straight narrative I had been expecting. In fact, bizarre as this may sound, it seems to me that you could make a case for Melville's being an experimental novelist. Rather than just spinning a tale from Ishmael's point of view, Melville is now jumping around from one POV to another. In these chapters, Ishmael, Ahab, Starbuck and Stubb all get to tell us their own thoughts. Isn't this the thing they always tell us not to do in writing classes – "Stick to a single point-of-view!"

Then talk to me about the chapters that read almost like play or film scripts, complete with stage directions! And naturally he has his science chapter (XXXI–"Cetology"). By now I'm kind of getting used to these science-of-whaling chapters, but I was surprised at the chapter on the cabin table meals. It read like something from a novel of manners or Emily Post. With so many different things happening in the book in terms of techniques, style and content, it's surprising that there's any room left over for anything to actually happen, for the story to move forward.

Maybe all this variety, all these side trips, all this fact-izing are why it is considered such a great book, "the one to beat." It's an ungainly patchwork of a novel that creates its effects and builds its volume by accretion, rather than by a straight-line, Conrad-like sea yarn. It's tough to get your arms around it, just when you think something's about to happen, you're off to Egypt as part of a history of the mast-head.

And just to keep the *Moby Dick* sightings going, we rented the reasonably lame romantic comedy *Alex & Emma* a few nights ago. In the movie Alex is an author and at one point he explains to Emma (Kate Hudson) the supreme importance of the first line in a novel. "Call me Ishmael" is quoted.

Over to you.

t.

April 17, 2004

Terry,

Are there no new ideas? I believe The Mosey was a new idea.

[When Steve and I were in junior high school there was a brief craze for hit songs tied to dances. "Hand Jive" by Johnny Otis and "The Stroll" by the Diamonds were perhaps the two most notable. Steve invented the name of a non-existent song patterned on this craze called "The Mosey." In our imagination it was recorded by an equally non-existent group called the Chesney Brothers, named after that year's third-string Michigan State quarterback. Armed

*with this mythical name, we would then call a radio request show
that supposedly based their weekly hit list on the volume of requests
and ask for "The Mosey" in an effort to try to get this non-existent
placed in the top ten. We never made it. TNH]*

Melville finishes his chapter on the science of whales by
declaring his work on the subject incomplete. He writes, "God keep
me from ever completing anything. This whole book is but a
draught----nay, but the draught of a draught."

And, so, indeed it is. This is not news to the reader of this book.
This book *Moby Dick* reads like a glistening, lumbering unfinished
work. Never quite tuned together. Never polished and delivered.
Just out there rough and not quite ready. This is impressive, this
book. But it is indeed incomplete. Imagine the work it would have
taken to complete it! Imagine the work! Imagine Melville staring at
all those pages strewn across his study. To bring it back to a single
point of view! To complete it! To shorten it, keeping only the best.
No, not Melville......rather have it be like a beast.

Ahab reveals that it is the whale *Moby Dick* who tore off his leg.
His passes wine, and fires the crew's brains up for revenge. (This
scene may have inspired the name of the 60s pop rock group Moby
Grape.)

(Prompted by the sudden remembrance of this group, I looked
them up. Fruit of research follows: "The band disintegrated, unable
to use the name which was owned by their manager, Matthew Katz
(b. 1929, Massachusetts, USA). The remaining members appeared
as Maby Grope, Mosley Grape, Grape Escape, Fine Wine, the
Melvilles, the Grape, the Hermans and the Legendary Grape.
During one of their many attempts at re-formation, two of the group
actually released a record as Fine Wine.")

Ahab is mad for revenge. The crew members are swept up by
his madness. But Starbuck does not buy in. To his still-water mind,
it's a ship set up to gather oil, not revenge.

In a way I cheer now for mad Captain Ahab simply because of
his energy, as I maybe would have cheered for Hitler if I was a

youth in Nazi Germany. I want Ahab to now go so crazy that he not only destroys the whale but the very book I'm reading.

Melville's characters ponder big violent philosophical issues throughout. But unlike Shakespeare's characters, who do the same, he does not have anyone ponder beautifully. Melville wants to use the force of his words to tear this beast of a book apart and hurl its bloody pieces around. This is not a book for boys, but it is not far enough from it. Nor is this book far enough from the Charles Bronson Death Wish movies about modern day urban revenge to be a great, deep, deliciously artful book. He interlaces religion, and religious symbolism. He reveals inner torment about what is and is not sacrilegious. It's a whirlwind of contrasting crew members' inner lives. But where is the joy and beauty in this book? Not a hint of it. And that, I believe, is what makes this book so difficult to love. So far.

You keep saying, and rightly, that *Moby Dick* is considered such a great book. But the question should be: do *we* consider it a great book? I believe reviewers and even society are intimidated by certain works and artists. Like Roger Ebert who absolutely cowers in the presence of Spike Lee.

Steve.

21 April 2004 – New York

Steve.

Fair point about the intimidation factor. I do think people get influenced by reputations and there is a certain amount of intellectual bullying that goes on. ("Shit, I hated this movie, but Orson Welles is well-known as brilliant, so I better say it's a masterpiece, otherwise people will think that *I'm* dumb.")

But I wonder what it was that made *Moby Dick* an acknowledged "great" novel in the first place. I remember reading somewhere that the book was not at all a success when it first hit the Barnes & Nobles of the 1850s – neither commercially *nor* critically. Sometime around 1920, however, there was a re-evaluation and it suddenly became the literary critics' darling. Why? Who? What did they see?

When we get back from Barcelona I'll do a bit of research and see if we can't get some of these questions answered. (We leave for Spain on April 30th and we'll be there for May and June; but as promised, I'll keep up my end of the *Moby Dick* studies and correspondence.)

Meanwhile I'll put out a hypothesis. Its towering reputation might have to do with the huge ambition of this novel, the way it tries, through all those literary side trips, to map the whole world of whaling, and beyond that, through parable and biblical references, the whole world period. Maybe it's the archetypical quality of the story that is valued. Note in your last letter, for instance, you compared elements of the novel to both *Death Wish* and Hitler. The whole epic nature of the vengeance tale lends itself to overlaying *Moby Dick* on any number of other situations. Try these:

1) First, one you alluded to. Hitler = Ahab. Germany/Hitler, materially and psychologically maimed by their defeat in World War I and the degrading terms of the Versailles Peace, is roused to a maniacal course of revenge by Hitler's inflammatory speeches and promise of regained glory.

2) George W. Bush = Ahab; Colin Powell = Starbuck; Saddam Hussein = Moby Dick. Bush, personally aggrieved by the attack on his father's reputation for not finishing off Hussein when he had the chance, becomes obsessed – to the point of irrationality – with hunting him down. Powell harbors private doubts. Etc.

3) The Red Sox = Ahab; Don Zimmer = Moby Dick. Unable to function sanely as a team because of the great wrongs done to them over the years by the Bronx Bombers, the Red Sox – led by Pedro Martinez – seek out the Yankee who most resembles a whale. Etc.

Perhaps it's this universality of analogical application that makes it such a great book. I think you could make a strong case for its being the all-time number one Revenge book – beating out *The Count of Monte Cristo, The Iliad* and *Hamlet*.

Last night we went to a performance of Larry Kramer's *The Normal Heart*. (Wait!, I have a question: are there any plays [I'm talking drama, not musicals] these days that are not about gays, the holocaust, blacks/Asians/immigrants or other versions of minority experience?) Anyway, here we are caught up in this pretty gripping play about the beginnings and dawning awareness of the AIDS epidemic in the early 1980s and, at one point, the lead character makes basically a gay pride speech in which he goes through a litany of names of the great gay men in history. The list is familiar: Plato, Aristotle, Oscar Wilde, Cole Porter, Walt Whitman and maybe ten or fifteen others; but what stunned me was the sudden appearance of the name "Herman Melville." His was the only name in this roll call of anyone I did not already know was gay – making me wonder why I didn't. I feel stupid. Did you know this? Is this common knowledge? Was I living in Europe when he was outed?

It certainly makes you look at the Ishmael/Queequeg night at the Spouter Inn scene in a different light. I think I'll have to research this also when I get back.

Finally. I've been so conscious of getting my *Moby Dick* impressions to you that I've neglected to thank you for your gifts, the Billy Collins book and the Hank Williams Tribute CD, which arrived more than a week ago. On the latter (which we've listened to a lot), I especially like the Sheryl Crow version of "Long Gone Lonesome Blues." The Collins book will go to Europe with me and I'll comment on it later.

How have you fared with the Jim Harrison/Ted Kooser poems I sent? Did you read the one I noted for you on page 37?

One of the interesting things about the leisurely way we're reading *Moby Dick* is that we're both obviously reading other books (and other *kinds* of books) over the same period. I find that I fall naturally into comparing. I'm not saying *Moby Dick* comes off any better or worse because of this. It's merely recognition of the fact that the things that are going on in our lives, and the things that are going on in our minds, clearly affect the perceptions of what we read. This exercise has interestingly made this point for me again.

This is hardly a new thought, I know.

It is, in fact, the reason why, to have an appreciation of Jack Kerouac, one *must* read him before the age of 21. Anyone who reads *On the Road* when old enough to vote comes away wondering how this drivel was ever considered literature. The same person can read the same book at 19 and at 40 and come away with two totally different impressions. Does this make sense? I think it does, but perhaps I chose a bad example.

Until the next ten chapters,

t.

1 May 2004 – Phoenix

Terry.

Starbuck's famous coffee shop chain took its name from the first mate aboard the ship, Starbuck. So *Moby Dick* is a major influence still in the culture … currently a play on Broadway, too.

But what is this all about?

Is there something wrong with me? I see a sprawling, almost insane book of undisciplined rants on the subject of evil, religion, symbols, revenge, and like, whoa what a drama queen! One early reviewer of Melville called him a "howling cheese."

Yet I am captivated as they launch small boats going after a whale and Queequeg hurls an errant harpoon and a boat capsizes showing us all how dangerous all of this is. How close death is. Why are we all doing this? So Ahab can get revenge for his lost leg? What would he have used it for? Soccer? Did he play soccer? (You can't use your hands in soccer).

Am I just kidding here? Why do people fear to lose their lives? What do they DO with their lives but wait for life to end anyway? Melville's search for meaning among the blubber and the waves is not fun for me, because it's so clumsy and crude. The characters are all confused it seems, and Melville sails on by making more of that confusion than simple low brain wattage. I say it's low brain wattage on the part of his narrator and crew, but Melville says it's profound. Sailor-philosophers pondering the human predicament.

I am reminded of the Jobim song sung by Sinatra that observes life as "a bitter tragic joke" (as also speculated by our narrator Ishmael). But what if you the reader do not agree with that viewpoint? Then this voyage into the seas against evil and fate is rather silly. A book for boys? No. Because boys know not to speculate on what life is, they just live it. They live it for God's sake, to the fullest. But poor insane Melville wrestles with all these questions from his sedentary, dark shadowy writer's study and the sensitive reader suffers.

Melville should have heeded Kierkegaard's advice (in my opinion, after having read up to chapter 50): "Above all, do not lose your desire to walk: every day I walk myself into a state of well-being and walk away from every illness; I have walked myself into my best thoughts, and I know of no thought so burdensome that one cannot walk away from it…but by sitting still, and the more one sits still, the closer one comes to feeling ill… Thus if one just keeps on walking, everything will be all right."

I conclude with some family album snapshots of the mixed-up Melvilles (maybe we can get Joyce Carol Oates to write *We Were the Mixed-Up Melvilles*): In 1867, after his literary reputation had waned, Melville's wife, Lizzie, was convinced that her husband was insane. Melville's father, Allen, suffered from dementia before his early death. When his son Malcolm killed himself at the age of 18, the coroner reported that it was "suicide by shooting himself with a pistol…under temporary insanity of Mind" Melville's remaining son, Stanwix, traveled aimlessly and insanely around the world, disappearing for a year in Central America before his death at age 35.

So clearly I've established that Herman was a drama queen; I suppose the open question now is: was he also a queen? Researching the sexual-orientation issue, I Googled my way to this from a forum on Camille Paglia's take on *Moby Dick*…interesting:

"Additionally, except for the blowsy woman who serves Ishmael chowder in the 2nd or 3rd chapter, there are NO women in this book. NONE. There is the memory of Captain Ahab's new bride at home, her head denting the pillow – but other than that – NO GIRLS. Although, if you look at the book in another light (as Camille Paglia does so brilliantly and so bizarrely in her chapter on it in Sexual Personae) – the whale could be seen as the "spirit" of female energy in the world. It is pretty obvious that the great white whale is a male, although it is never specifically said – but Paglia made me see something else going on. Whaling boats were 100% male, they lived out on the ocean for 3 or 4 years at a time. There were no women. None.

"Melville himself was an unrepentant and vicious misogynist. He tried to kill his wife. She would flee from the house in the night, screaming, etc. It is well known that he had many homosexual experiences during his time at sea. Many whalers did.

"Paglia believes that Melville was writing out his anxiety and his anger towards women, in general. But not just "women" as in "a person who happens to be female," but on a larger level: Woman as nature, woman as chaos, woman as the uncontrollable force running the universe."

Paglia feels that the entire book, with basically not one woman in it, is actually haunted by this spectre of female-ness. As I said, interesting.

Finally, related to whaling, I know I've mentioned my desire not to become one, and the diet I've embarked upon to avoid that happening. Actually my goal – my determination—is to get back to my high school weight of 175. But tell me again about how your diet worked. Wasn't it 1000 calories a day? Tell me you have arrived and are safe and happy in Barcelona. Then tell me about your 1,000-calorie day system.

I just did a 1,000-calorie day yesterday. I am now down 9 pounds in my journey.

Here's what I put into a 1,000-calorie day:
celery
apples
banana
whole wheat toast dry
hard boiled egg
small can of tuna
low fat jello
carrot

s.

5 Mayo 2004 – Barcelona (chapters 41-50)

Steve.

I'm afraid this is later than I had promised, and as you pointed out in one of your books, one should not make promises and then not keep them. To be honest, this particular little suggestion had been made to me at a much younger age. Still, knowing what's right and doing right are two different things as everyone who's ever stepped into a confession box can attest.

Jet lag seems to affect me more than it used to and I have dragged through the first few days here. Barcelona is as beautiful and lively as I remember it; the weather, however, has been ugly, dark gray clouds, rainy and chilly. But from the balcony of our sixth floor apartment, we can actually see the Sea a long walk to the south. I feel certain that the famous Mediterranean weather is just around the corner.

(I note in the IHT that you've been having 100-degree days the last few. Been out to a ball game yet? What a strange team you have this year. They remind me of the late-80s/early 90s Tigers, who I always figured that if they scored ten runs in a game had about a 50-50 chance of winning.)

We are located a few blocks from Gaudi's Sagrada Familia. We look north to the green hills of the Collserola. And right below us there is a small park, which we look down on, with a statue of a man called Anton Clave holding a conductor's baton at the ready. Clave was apparently a very big deal in the choral music game. I mention this last because I seem to recall that your brother-in-law – and also your wife? – were choral music people and I thought that maybe this distant connection with Clave would raise you in their estimation. Then again, maybe not.

On to a more pressing matter: the question of Melville's sexual preferences and their effect on the novel. I admit that it's true that in 1851 it would have been literary suicide – though definitely a daring and courageous move – for Melville to decide to write the first overtly gay novel and thus give birth to whole bookstore sections devoted to trade paperbacks with covers featuring buff guys with short, peroxided hair and wearing tank tops. 1851 was definitely too early for that breakthrough: 1951 was probably still too early. But it still seems a bit of a leap to me that contemporary critics would analyze the novel as being crypto-homosexual.

I mean, so there are no women in the novel. How many women were there on those whaling ships anyway? If you had spent a couple of years at sea on a whaler and wanted to write a novel about it, wouldn't you balk at artificially including a couple of female characters in the book merely for the sake of establishing credentials for agenda-oriented close-readers from a century-and-a-half in the future?

Paglia, in her own way, is as much of a monomaniac as Ahab, and just as unreliable. Perhaps it's my law school experience, though I suspect it's just my natural inclination, but I value the rational, balanced view. I don't say this proudly, because in fact I think I miss a lot by not being more headlong and have at times made an effort to throw caution to the winds, but in the end I always feel more comfortable with the state of equilibrium. I will say, however, that it's always more interesting reading the sensationalists and the unbalanced.

So here's my take: I think *Moby Dick* (so far anyway) is a book about whaling. It's also a book about revenge and religion and maybe even about the nature of good and evil. But I simply don't see it as a 600-page metaphor for cruising Christopher Street. I say this based on the evidence of the text and regardless of whether Melville was actually gay or not. In fact, I find the book much more in the vein of what the English called "Lad Lit," which is the male version of "Chick Lit" epitomized by *Bridget Jones Diary*.

On the more interesting underlying question of whether Melville was gay or not, I'm coming down on the side of no. I say this based on personal experience. I've known a lot of gay men. Some I've liked: some I haven't. But none of them have bored me.

I'd like to submit the evidence of chapter 42 "The Whiteness of the Whale" as conclusive proof that Herman was straight as a harpoon. It took me hours to get through that chapter because I kept falling asleep. I mean it was tough slogging. Sometimes I'd only make it through a half sentence before the old ojos would close again.

(Have you heard of an artist named Robert Ryman? He's a well-known American painter from Nashville originally. [The Ryman Auditorium is somehow connected with his family.] Several years ago there was a retrospective of his work at the Museum of Modern Art in New York. It was more than forty years of work and it was entirely white. Personally I would have gotten bored after a couple of years and maybe branched out into a light gray or something, but Ryman stuck with it. And that I suppose is what has made him the art legend he is today, that dogged persistence. On seeing this show I was naturally struck by the genius of his work, but now, I begin to suspect that at some point in his sophomore year at Nashville Central High School, or wherever, Ryman was assigned *Moby*

Dick. Unlike either of us in high school, he managed to get to chapter 42 "The Whiteness of the Whale" and, even more amazingly, he managed to get through the chapter. "Here it is," he must have said in a eureka moment, "I've found my life's work!" The rest is history.)

And yet, just a few chapters later we're lowering boats to go chase whales and I'm totally caught up in the chase. That whole sequence really captured the adventure yarn quality that I had thought would be the hallmark of the entire book. A great section, didn't you think?

Anyway, I'm back on track now. My next section will be early, I promise, so this time you can respond to me.

terry.

May 6, 2004 – Phoenix

Terry.

I must admit I do not know Anton Clave, the man behind your Barcelona statue, by name, but your memory of my association with choral groups is quite right. I have spent many hours watching not only my wife sing in chorus, but also her brother sing in the Orpheus Men's Chorus. Notably, they have released a CD of sea shanties that might make a glorious CD to put into the back cover flap of this book! On that CD of sea songs there is the classic shanty, "Blow the Man Down" and it occurs to me that it might as well have been written by *Moby Dick* the whale about Ahab our captain when it says:

> There was an old skipper I don't know his name
> With a way, hey, blow the man down
> Although he once played a remarkable game
> Give me some time to blow the man down.

Bye.

Steve

7 mayo 2004 – Barcelona

steve.

We finally got a decent break on the weather here yesterday, so we spent the afternoon wandering around a neighborhood called Barceloneta down by the sea. Lunch was a fabulous squid-ink-drenched paella and white wine outdoors overlooking the Mediterranean. And yet, though I've painted a picture of lazy indulgence, my mind was ablaze. It was not a very organized fire I must admit, but I kept having little *Moby Dick* thoughts or thinking of comments responding to your last few e-mails. I was without a pen and I had to borrow Miranda's to jot all these things down so I wouldn't forget them.

This morning naturally some of these things don't seem as urgent or brilliant. Still, I took the trouble to note them, so you're going to get a pageful. I am assuming that if one can give someone an "earful," then, in writing, one can give a pageful – or, to be more properly parallel, perhaps it should be an eyeful (but then this has much different connotations).

Did the coffee people really get their name from the Pequod's first mate? Have you read that or heard it somewhere? And, if it's true (I have often wondered), then what aspect of this stalwart's character did these Seattle marketers think made his the perfect name for their ubiquitous chain?

The Starbucks' phenomenon is widely hated here in Barcelona, at least in conversation. It's seen as yet another tentacle in the octopus called globalization, or more accurately, Americanization. And yet, I've seen maybe four Starbucks here so far and the places are jammed. They can't all be American tourists.

I absolutely love the concept of Melville's being a "howling cheese." As a matter of fact, I just love the concept period. I know that at 59 this may be a foolhardy ambition, but I am going to marshal my remaining forces and the bag of tricks experience has given me and point them all in the direction of attaining howling cheese status for myself. Is this silly? Is it too late? Like Zelda Fitzgerald deciding at 30 that she wanted to be a dancer when she should have started at least 15-20 years earlier?

You rail against Melville's "undisciplined rants": I question his sociological (the ship's hierarchy and on-board meal decorum), transcendental (the contemplation of white) and scientific (the classification of the whale family) side trips. But it all reminds me of a definition of "the novel" that I once read: "a book of fiction of a certain length that has something wrong with it." Presumably a *great* novel must be a work of fiction with a *great deal* wrong with it. Perhaps this is how *Moby Dick* made the Hall of Fame.

You say the characters are confused. I think Melville has made the reader confused, not the characters. In fact, I see the characters, with the exception of Ishmael, as being very straightforward almost simple. The only one who's doing any questioning of the meaning of life (or of white, for that matter) is Ishmael. The reader, on the other hand, has no idea what he's reading: an economic treatise? A metaphysical exploration? A zoology text? A novel? Dickens (a pretty close contemporary) never pulled this shit.

You quoted the Jobim song on life being "a bitter tragic joke." Compare Ishmael referring to God as "the unseen and unaccountable old joker" at the beginning of chapter 49. And you tell me this guy is not the equal of Jobim! In the same vein, one of my favorite books (four books actually) is Lawrence Durrell's the Alexandria Quartet; in it there is a character who is a novelist (Pursewarden) who has written an acclaimed trilogy called *God is a Humourist*. (You'll pardon the English spelling; the author was English.)

And now on to the weightier question of shedding pounds. I'm afraid I have nothing to tell you that you don't already know. All I can impart is how I do it (to the extent I do it):

It's straight mathematics. There is nothing magical about it. 3500 calories equals a pound. Your body burns a certain number of calories each day just in normal activities. This number varies based on your weight. According to weight charts I've seen, at 175 pounds my body burns 2700 calories or something like that. Miranda's body, at 115 pounds, only burns 1800 calories, which she finds very unfair. The other unfair thing in this comparison is that Miranda actually weighs 115, while I weigh 181 (or did when I left New York; it's been unfettered eating since I've been here). But since I *want* to weigh 175, I set my calorie burning level there because that's what I'll have to maintain once I get there.

So in theory if I consume 2800 calories every day, at the end of 35 days I'll gain a pound. If, on the other hand, I consume 2600 calories a day, at the end of 35 days I'll lose one pound. I look on these as the absolutes.

So then, here was my system. Given the inexact nature of calorie counting, I lower my maintenance ration to 2500. Then each day I counted calories. For every 500 calories I was under 2500, I gave myself a star. So, you mention a 1000-calorie day; that would be a three star day for me. If I consumed 1300 calories, I'd give myself two stars. And so on.

I marked the stars on my pocket calendar. Every seven stars equals 3500 calories equals a pound. The short term swings of two or three pounds on the scale don't really matter. It is the unerring mathematics of the star count that is the real result. Over time, you lose in pounds whatever the total is of the calories you don't eat divided by 3500.

All of this is based on absolute, irrefutable fact. Where it falls apart is lack of discipline on the part of the dieter. The things that I found that screwed me up were dinners out, traveling, entertaining clients and boredom with the detail and the routine of counting calories. Success in any discipline involves the ability to keep interested. And it's not easy. After a couple of days, one is tempted to say: okay this calorie counting is a pain, but it's not that bad, I can do this. But that's after only a few days. If you want to lose, say, thirty pounds, you're looking at keeping interested for about five months or 150 days. (This is based on 10-star weeks, which is generally what I aim for.)

These are the basics of the system I've used off and on for over a decade now. And it *always* works. Or, I guess I should say, it always works to the extent I'm able to hold up my end on the discipline side. This last time I modified the system somewhat just to help keep it interesting to me and to accommodate our travel schedule, but at bottom it's still based on the same immutable mathematical certainties.

t.

9 May 2004 – Phoenix

t.

Glad you're weighing in on the gay issue. And I do agree with you. I once had a friend in Berlin to whom I said one night when we were in our cups, "You're gay aren't you?" and he said, "No, I'm sicker than that." And I believe that is true of Melville.

You are spot-on about the novel being about whaling and revenge and religion. I even think it's revenge against religion. Or, at least, against the broken promise of religion. Melville makes a common angry intellectual's mistake (let's call him an intellectual because in his day he was one, in this day and age he would be marginal) in raging against a particularly narrow and contracted form of spirituality (the preacher in the earlier chapter bellowing moronically about judgment day).

The promise of the spirit is not broken simply because you cannot find it in that one antiquated, misguided, myth-drunk church. That would be like saying that literature is overrated and indeed worthless because you read a Dean Koontz novel once and found it to be vulgar and lame. Or: "I don't like poetry. I read Rod McKuen once and that was it for me."

I find in Melville arrested emotional development. I find it in Norman Mailer, too, but in Mailer it doesn't matter because he is so brilliant and such an artist with words. He's so funny, you just don't care. (Approaching Anthony Burgess at a cocktail party, Mailer drunkenly yells, "Your last book was shit, Burgess!" In his social life Mailer had made himself a kind of caricature of Mailer. He was Mailer as Mailer would be on South Park or The Simpsons.)

In Melville, though, you care. You care about that arrested emotional development because you are paying for it with every page you turn. In fact, I think we can attribute a fair per cent of the high school dropout rate over the past fifty years to this man.

And on the name Starbuck's as used by the Seattle latte-meisters: although various urban legends swirl about the origin of the name of the coffee chain, the owners admit that the *Moby Dick* character is the indirect source.

Steve

12 May 2004 – Phoenix

terry.

Let's look at these chapter titles for 55, 56 and 57: "Of the Monstrous Pictures of Whales"; "Of the Less Erroneous Pictures of Whales, and the True Pictures of Whaling Scenes"; "Of Whales in Paint; In Teeth; In Wood; In Sheet-Iron; In Stone; In Mountains; In Stars." This is a digression into the art world, a digression that features an observation by Ishmael that the whale is "the one creature in the world which must remain unpainted to the very last," since with the exception of actually going whaling in person "there is no earthly way of finding out precisely what the whale really looks like."

In other words, these chapters hold no real value to the reader, but Melville felt that he went to all the trouble to do the art research so "they're going in there! The reader be damned!"

For symbols I prefer poetry to Melville. I prefer Amy Lowell and the Imagists. Now they could give you exciting and aesthetically pleasing symbols in writing. But Melville's symbols, (Does the whale represent the false allure of conquerable evil? Does the sea represent the unfathomed psyche? Does the code of honor & revenge among whalers represent man's inability to live a religion? Or what?), Melville's symbols begin to symbolize his own confused state.

Melville writes "as this appalling ocean surrounds the verdant land, so in the soul of man there lies one insular Tahiti, full of peace and joy, but encompassed by all the horrors of the half-known life."

This calls to mind Colin Wilson's observation that "all philosophy is biography in disguise." Certainly this seems true of Melville. A tormented man downloads his poison into a clumsy, gargantuan book. The book becomes required reading. The book is very famous, but who has actually read all of it? Soon, you and I. We will be the first two. We can tell the world how it ends. I doubt if the world knows. How could it? No one is known to have finished it.

s.

13 mayo 2004 – Barcelona (Chapters 51-60)

Steve.

This stretch of ten chapters sums up at once both why I am so baffled by the exalted reputation the book enjoys and why I'm liking it so much as a totally quirky piece of work. In these ten chapters, the story was advanced by inches. In fact in only two or three of the chapters in this ten-chapter stretch do any of the characters in the book even appear. And yet we are dealt yards and yards of atmosphere and background. The whole thing is like a patchwork quilt pieced together around the few threads of the story.

We not only get a side story about the Erie Canal men that really has only the most tenuous connection to our story, but of all things, we get the survey of whale art. I have come to expect chapters on zoology and others on the technical details of whaling, so the giant squid and grazing habits of the right whale chapters, plus the one on rope didn't faze me in the slightest. I find these chapters curious and I find it interesting that Melville unloads them on us. What is he thinking? But my question is how did the literary establishment, usually so fussy about the form and structure of a novel, allow *Moby Dick* to pass Go?

So maybe, I thought, this formlessness was simply the convention of the time and all the novels written in the mid-1800s were this odd collage of bits of information, stories, research, philosophizing and whatever else pops into the author's head. But this theory doesn't really hold up. Not that I've read a whole lot of mid-1800's novelists, but I have read all of Hawthorne's novels and not one of them is remotely like this in structure.

Maybe the whole thing is like a baseball game. You know how they say that in a great nine-inning game that lasts two and a half hours, there's actually only eleven minutes of actual action? And yet without the other two hours and nineteen minutes, it's not really a great baseball game.

Well, in 550 pages of *Moby Dick* I suggest that there are maybe 150 pages of story, but maybe without the other 400 pages you don't have "The Great American Novel."

You did not comment, so perhaps you did not think it odd, but unless there was a typo in your e-mail of the first of May, it would appear that Melville had a son named Stanwix. You've tended to produce mainly girls so you've not had to wrestle as much with the question of whether to name a son Stanwix or not. But let me assure you it's a real conundrum. With both my sons I had to grapple long with the pros and cons of the name.

In favor, of course, is that you wind up with a son named Stanwix. But the negative side is that, on hearing your son's name, people are always saying, "Oh, that is *so* Herman Melville," with a dismissive air that immediately signals their categorization of you as one of those who simply follows the crowd.

In the end, in the instances of both my sons, obviously, I decided against the name. Do I have regrets? Well naturally, but one must learn to put those things in the past. Ever forward! That's my motto.

(I also hedged my bet, as you know, by giving Lincoln the middle name of Starbuck. For this act, he has, perhaps properly, never forgiven me. I wonder if I can gain his absolution if I let him know that Stanwix was also in the running.)

Why is the discipline of losing weight so much more difficult than any other? You have quit drinking and I have quit smoking so we both have shown some degree of self-discipline and yet losing weight is constantly a question of advances and backslides. I suspect the reason is the unabsolute nature of the discipline involved.

You quit drinking by saying you would not have a drop of alcohol. When I quit smoking I denied myself even a single cigarette. In losing weight, however, clearly you don't have the option of not allowing yourself food. So the whole process is one of compromise. You can eat this; but not that. You can have this; but only half a portion. If you have that can of Coke; you'll have to ride the exercise bike for twenty minutes.

This is why to lose weight you have to surrender to the tyranny of the numbers. If you live by the numbers, you will lose by the numbers. You cannot lose weight by saying, "I will eat less today." That's too vague. You lose weight by saying: "I will consume only 1000 calories today." You are not eating a three-egg, cheese omelet; you are counting 350 calories. The unabsolute nature of dieting is also why I invent absolutes to incorporate into my discipline. (e.g. I will not *drink* a calorie. Or, for a month, not a single potato chip. No bread at a restaurant. Etc.)

I will say that I think you are a little over ambitious in trying to get down to your high school weight. Your body wasn't fully developed at that time. I'd think your ideal, fit weight today would be somewhere around 185-190. Your goal of 175 strikes me as impossible. Which is, of course, what will make it so great when you do it.

You also earlier asked the question as to whether Ahab had played soccer (or, over here, "futbol"). I've done a bit of internet research and can find no reference to Ahab's ever having played "the beautiful game." (By the way, I just looked *that* up and find that the quote is attributed to Pele.)

But the point is, if he had given up the sea and turned to soccer after his accident, Ahab would have had a far different fate than the image of the monomaniacal revenge-seeker to which he's been consigned. He would have been the subject of made-for-TV movies, a symbol of courage, determination and redemption.

"But the guy only had one leg," you say? You have obviously forgotten Lou Brissie. He was the Ahab of Major League Baseball. He only had one leg (lost the other in WWII, I believe) and yet he pitched a number of years in the majors with the Philadelphia

Athletics. He was the John Swainson of the mound.

[John Swainson was the Democratic Governor of Michigan while Steve and I were in high school. He had lost both his legs in World War II. I vividly remember a high school Civics class in which Steve's teacher leading a discussion of current events had asked who the class thought were likely candidates for the gubernatorial election that year. Someone suggested Swainson, to which Steve immediately said, "Swainson can't run." "Why not, Steve?" asked the Civics teacher. "He doesn't have any legs," Steve replied.

The phrase "politically correct" had not been coined back then, but the concept was understood and obviously Steve was in for a major rebuke from the teacher. The rebuke was duly delivered though it would have carried a lot more weight if the teacher had been able to keep from laughing. TNH]

I don't have access to historical baseball stats here, Steve, so would you do me a favor and look Brissie up. I'd be interested in his pitching record, but what I'd really like to know is if he ever stole a base.

And while we're on the subject of futbol: I have a wonderful writing studio here with French windows opening out to a balcony overlooking the wide boulevard of Passeig de Sant Joan. The only drawback is the attractive, even seductive, collection of books housed here. Stymied by a particularly reluctant sentence, it's too easy to get sidetracked by picking up a book and losing myself in it for a time. As everywhere, however, side trips often have their serendipitous rewards. Consider this Jean-Paul Sartre quote on soccer I found:

"In a football match everything is complicated by the presence of the opposite team."

No wonder the man was considered brilliant.

By the way, I hope you are still planning on coming to Andrew's wedding in Halifax in September. Not only will it give you a taste of a real sea-faring town, but – according to the schedule – we should have just finished *Moby Dick* that week. We can have a nice gam.

[Gam is a word that comes straight from Moby Dick where it is, in fact, defined in chapter 53 as "a social meeting of two or more whaleships, generally on a cruising ground; when, after exchanging hails, they exchange visits by boats' crews." TNH]

tnh.

14 May 2004 – Phoenix

terry.

Actually, what Sartre is most known for is taking neutral, meaningless situations and imbuing them with negative connotations. He is also known for taking good situations and nihilistically rendering them neutral. He is a perfect example of the thought that "all philosophy is biography." One good thing was that the wall-eyed Sartre (don't ever order that in a French restaurant, they'll be offended) may have been the inspiration for the popular American TV series Columbo.

Life is numbers. People who wake up to that become happy. People who DUCK the numbers end up like Enron or Ariel Sharon.

[I had several weeks earlier sent Steve a newspaper photo of Ariel Sharon looking like an over-inflated Macy's Thanksgiving Parade balloon float. TNH]

And yes, you are right about the non-absoluteness of weight-loss discipline, but there are other difficulties too. You also have to start anew every day … bargain with yourself … make potentially humiliating promises to friends and relatives, etc …

I am now 10 pounds down on the way to "Forever Birmingham" weight.

["Forever Birmingham" was our high school alma mater song. This is a reference to Steve's goal to get down to his high school weight. TNH]

And I take your point on the fact that the body was not fully developed but I'm going there anyway. I can't tell you how many pro football cards I have had of running backs where the guy was 5-11, 175. It's not that skinny is it really? Tell me.

"No man in the world has more courage than the man who can stop after eating one peanut."

—*Channing Pollock*

s.

15 May 2004 – Barcelona

Steve.

Since the start of the book I have been longing for a good discussion of the bones in the whale's side fin. I'm sure you have shared this desire. And then, right there in the second-to-the-last paragraph in Chapter 55, Herman delivers. Not only that, he immediately follows it up with this reference to the mitten-like structure of the side fin:

"'However recklessly the whale may sometimes serve us,' said the humorous Stubbs one day, 'he can never be truly said to handle us without mittens.'"

Stubbs just cracks me up.

Regarding your comments on the "art" chapters. Have you ever read a book called *The Alienist* by Caleb Carr. It's kind of a mystery/thriller that takes place in New York in the late 1800s. It was a big success a few years back so I read it to see what all the hullabaloo was about. I felt about it much as you feel about *Moby Dick*. There were just too many sections where I felt like saying, "Caleb, your research is showing!" Long passages having nothing to do with the story and everything to do with time spent in the library.

How old do you see Ahab as? He's probably supposed to be younger than I picture him, but I can't help thinking of him as an old guy. And you know, it kind of makes me root for him a bit. Is this a sign of my own age? I have noticed for some time now I have been rooting for the old guys in sports. For instance, I've never really been a big Roger Clemens fan; he's a bit over the top for me. But now, even though he left the Yankees, I am pulling for him to cop just one more Cy Young Award. Who is the oldest guy ever to win one? I don't think anyone's won one in his 40s, or frankly anywhere close. I don't know, maybe Randy Johnson. But if the season ended today, Roger'd win it hands down. A 7-0 record and an ERA around 2.00. No one else would get a vote. *[In November of 2004, Roger Clemens, who ended the season 18-4 with a 2.98 ERA, was awarded his 7th Cy Young Award. TNH]*

And finally this from Barcelona. In most restaurants here the desert menu includes something called "Music." Isn't that delightful. ("I think I'll just have a little music for dessert.") Of course we had no idea what it actually was so we employed our usual system for finding out what mystery dishes are – we ordered it.

Music, it turns out, is a medley of various nuts, served with a small glass of dessert wine. It's not at all bad and we've ordered it several times now. But somehow it had more romance to it when I didn't know what it was and it was just "Music." At that time, it also seemed the ideal low-cal dessert option.

t.

16 May 2004 – Phoenix

terry.

I'm down 11 pounds since the beginning of my *crusade* (I, like most Republicans, enjoy violent Christian references when anticipating success in ANY field.)

What if the whole world were talking me out of losing weight? What if everyone was saying, "Can I buy you lunch?" and "Ready for dinner?" and food had become a big social thing. What if the ads between innings were about food and drink? What if there was a fast food joint on every corner? What if the movie theaters made all their money not on tickets but on the snacks? What if?

Then to set a goal and reach it, especially a profound goal and reach it, would be something.

On old guys:I believe seniors should get no drugs whatsoever, and should not be allowed to retire. In fact I believe we should increase the workday for seniors and give them all the jobs we are now giving the illegal aliens. We should require that seniors learn Spanish and speak it in the fields. That would be my program if I ran for president. That and the elimination of handicapped parking. PLUS: The death penalty for attempted suicide.

But I cheer for older guys, too…I cheer for Ahab because he has a game going on. Ishmael does not. Ishmael is a philosopher, which is to say that he, like Melville, is a head case (in sports lingo.) I don't like Clemens personally. He's like one of those headstrong guys in school that I always hated … a bully to Piazza's sensitive boy … I would have been friends with Piazza and hated Clemens. Clemens takes himself way too seriously. For my taste, I prefer Jim Bouton. I prefer Greg Maddux, even.

Steve.

17 May 2004 – Barcelona

Steve.

First off, congratulations on the eleven pounds you've lost so far. (What is your current weight, by the way?) But now I want to point out the fact that you've lost it too quickly. In other words, the number of calories you've *not* eaten doesn't equal 38,500 yet, right?

So, as pleased as you are by your progress thus far, it is – to some extent – faux. This is what we call the "Beginning Bounce." (When I say "we" I'm talking about those of us who have attained diet-meister status.) This is not to take away from the minus-eleven, it only means that sometime in the near future you will hit a plateau (you may even register a gain) and even though you are toting up non-calories in the thousands, it will not show on the scale.

You cannot allow yourself to get discouraged by this. In the end, the numbers never lie.

I might add that you have greater motivation than most people to stick to the discipline and lose the weight. I mean, you make your living as a motivator, as a self-help guru. If you can't manufacture enough motivation to get yourself down to your playing weight, then why would any sane person pay you to help them achieve their goals? It is not just your self-image on the line; it's your livelihood.

Maddux is my man too, as you know. And I would much prefer him to win another Cy Young than Clemens. For one thing, I love the way Maddux has done it all with guile and control and Clemens with a 99 mph fastball and a mad-dog attitude. I long for Maddux to have another 15-game-winning season and recently his pitching hasn't been bad so he might just get it.

But if the Cy Young comes down to Clemens versus some 22-year-old Achilles who doesn't yet know that in another couple of decades he's going to have to pass up that piece of cheesecake and have hair on his shoulders and quite possibly also a heel problem, I'm rooting for Clemens.

t.

18 May 2004 – Phoenix

Terry.

    "too quickly"? What do you mean by this? Your original theory is that this is pure math, but now, like Einstein mixing space and time into a continuum, you've introduced a new factor into the formula – "too quickly." According to the math of calories, one loses according to the math ... YES, in the two months I've been at this I have created the necessary deficit ... some days just doing 1,000 (easier than I thought) and many days 1500. You are right: my travel schedule (which is extensive – I am in at least one other city at least once a week) makes it easy to go off. Eating as Dr. Phil says, for "emotional reasons" "Whaaat you've cancelled my flight home? I'll take two quarter-pounders with cheese while I process this upset."

    ALSO: many of my clients, especially CEO types, love to have long working lunches. And I cover my anxiety over how to diplomatically talk to them about the errors of their ways by saying "PASS THOSE FRIES THERE'S SOMETHING I NEED TO CONFRONT YOU ON!"

    Einstein said that we were stupid to think of time and space as separate entities. And that those of us who continued to do so would have to accept the consequences. String Theory resolves Einstein's breakthrough work with Quantum physics but posits a slew of new dimensions to make it all fit. You get the same feeling that you get in a poker game when the dealer starts announcing a long string of cards that are, for this one game, WILD.

s.

19 Mayo 2004 – Barcelona

steve.

You are reading me carelessly. I have not introduced anything new. I said the numbers never lie and I stick by that. The bathroom scale, however, does lie. My point is do not let unexplainable weight variations (as measured by the scale) discourage you from staying the course.

Secondly, you're right; if you have actually forgone 38,500 calories during the last two months, then your 11-pound loss is legit. I simply hadn't realized you've been at this for two months. I was thinking it was just the last three weeks or so.

So, I ask again, how much do you weigh now?

And this brings up an interesting point in Melville's *Whaling 101.* In all that scientific download Herm gives us, all the vomiting of index cards onto the printed page, have you once come across a mention of the actual size of a whale, in terms of feet or yards, or weight in pounds? I can't remember one. So why has he withheld this information from us?

I suppose I am stuck on my point of Melville's unloading all this very detailed whaling information and folklore in the book because it is so very different from what I expected. Like you, I expected the unraveling of a yarn. I find many of these little whaling essays interesting in themselves, but even more I find all of this "non-fiction" fascinating as a way of structuring a novel.

Look at it this way: bullfighting. Now, you know I am not a huge Hemingway fan, but consider this. He wrote a book that is in some ways a "bullfighting" novel – *The Sun Also Rises*. It's about 250 pages. He also wrote a non-fiction book on bullfighting called *Death in the Afternoon*, which is maybe 350 pages and loaded with the same kind of detailed, technical information about bullfighting that Melville tells us about whaling.

So, now let's say I'm Hemingway's manager/agent and, to make things even more unrealistic, let's say that I (as the agent) had read *Moby Dick*. So here's our conversation:

HEMINGWAY:

So screw the sales, Kid. The money is good and it buys the wine, which is good and splendid and makes you sleepy and horny at the same time. But the money is nothing next to the conflict.

ME:

What conflict, Papa?

HEMINGWAY:

The war between the man and the book. The campaign to write the Great American Novel and win the Nobel Prize.

ME:

Yeah, the Nobel means a lot of money.

HEMINGWAY:

[Obscenity] the money! I want the conflict, the struggle; I want Melville's crown! (And, of course, the Nobel. But not for the money!)

ME:

Okay. You want the title? Here's how you get it. You know those two books you've written, The Sun Also Rises and the bullfighting non-fiction one?

HEMINGWAY:

Yeah.

ME:

Put them together. Quit looking so goggle-eyed! Put them together into one book.

HEMINGWAY:

How?

ME:

It doesn't really matter. Alternate chapters or just shuffle the pages. Give the reader a chapter of story and Stallone dialogue and then give them a factual chapter on the intricacies of the matador's cape-work.

HEMINGWAY:

But that would mean that the book would have no shape. It would be an ungainly, clanging mess; it would even be sprawling. Plus it would be over 600 pages long!

ME:

Papa, have you ever *read Moby Dick?*

HEMINGWAY:

I got a B on the test on it.

ME:

That wasn't what I asked. Have you *read* it?

HEMINGWAY:

What's the point of reading the [obscenity] book – I mean, the [obscenity] thing is over 600 [obscenity] pages long. Besides. I know the story. I saw the movie with Gregory Peck.

Hemingway ignores my advice and continues his attempt to go 15 rounds with Melville. At first he decides that the problem is that he hasn't written a long book. So he writes a long war book – this one starring Gary Cooper. No Nobel. Finally he comes back to me in desperation.

HEMINGWAY:

Okay, Kid, maybe I should have listened to you the first time. But now I'm getting old. The legs are going. I figure I got maybe one more shot. I'll do whatever you tell me – just get me that Nobel.

ME:

Anything?

HEMINGWAY:

Yeah, just tell me what to do.

ME:

Go home and write a book about a man going out to sea to catch a big fish. Catching the fish becomes a maniacal passion with this guy.

HEMINGWAY:

Wait, you're saying I should re-write *Moby Dick*?

ME:

No, it doesn't have to be about whaling. But it has
to be about the men and the sea and the chase and
courage and maybe Joe DiMaggio.

HEMINGWAY:

DiMaggio? You gone nuts, Kid?

ME:

Look, Papa, at the risk of future copyright
infringement: Just Do It!

HEMINGWAY:

Okay, okay, but I'm not the Papa I used to be, you
know. I can't go 600 pages any more.

ME:

How many can you go?

HEMINGWAY:

Maybe a hundred ... large type.

ME:

That should be enough.

Well, the rest is history. Of course, he never thanked me – the
[obscenity]!

And while I'm on the subject of immortality, let me just register this before it becomes common knowledge. Smarty Jones is not a great horse. He may be undefeated, he may even win the Triple Crown, but he ain't a great horse.

His first six wins were in low-rent districts. And while both his Derby and Preakness wins have been impressive (though I only read about the Preakness, which is not considered a major event here), the times have been below average. He can be fully excused for the slow-motion Derby because the track was a sea of mud. But in the Preakness, no matter how much people talk about the move he put on at the head of the stretch, the time was not great

Simple as this – it's a bad year for 3-year-olds. Later in the year when Smarty has to face horses from other years – 4- and 5-year-olds – we'll find out that he's just a pretty good horse. Certainly, with all the money he's won, he´s better than an empty stall, but in the end, just a pretty good horse that caught a bad year just right.

t.

21 Mai 2004 – Salon de Province (the home of Nostrodamos)

(Chapters 61-70)

steve.

I am sitting on the terrace of a dowdy little café in a beautiful, sunny square here in this small Provençal town. Next to me, about to be opened, is *Moby Dick*. It is my traveling copy so I will put my finger in my espresso and make my mark on the title page and send it on to you that you might have a taste of Southern France in May. (Yes, I am aware that this last sounds like one of those Jim Harrison I'm-getting-old-so-I-see-miracles-in-the-quotidian poems.)

We drove up here yesterday for the wedding of friends from Paris. His father is France's ambassador to the UN (obviously not much liked by your pal Bush) so we've also seen them several times in New York when they come to visit. It's been four years since we've spent any time in the South of France so we're making a week of it.

Our goal in life is to be given the prize for furthest-traveled at every wedding we attend, but I am sincerely hoping you and Kathy will break our string on September 4th in Halifax, N.S., at Andrew's wedding.

And now on to *Moby Dick*.

These last ten chapters contain, I believe, the key to Melville's true objective in writing *Moby Dick*. For more than 400 pages now he's been drowning us in whalabilia, letting us know just how much of an expert he is on the subject of whaling. But to what end?

In chapter 62 though, he gives himself away. For there, while describing the pattern of operation in the small boat while chasing and harpooning the whale, he puts forward a couple of recommendations for changing that operation: A) Don't tire the harpooner by making him row the boat, and B) Eliminate the practice of the boatheader and the harpooner changing places when the whale starts to run. ("Foolish and unnecessary.")

Now what does this sound like? It seems clear to me that Melville was angling for a job as a whaling consultant. The man obviously recognized that there was no real money in being a novelist and he wanted to get a job with McKinsey or Andersen Consulting (aka Accenture) in the Whaling Practice.

I mean the cheek – the sheer gall – of this dilettante whaler saying: No, no, no, gentlemen, you've been doing it all wrong; let me put you back on course. This is, naturally, exactly what consultants do every day. And the big benefit for Melville would be that he could charge by the hour instead of hoping his books might sell.

Among the mates, Stubb is much my favorite. I should have given Lincoln the middle name of Stubb instead of Starbuck. Starbuck is necessary, of course, stalwart, serious and all business, but Stubb, now there's a man for a bit of a laugh. (I have no feelings one way or the other on Flask, the third mate.)

Today, Stubb would have his own television show I feel certain. He must have had the crew in stitches with his merciless ribbing of the cook: instructing him in the fine art of cooking a whale steak, and making him harangue the sharks about making so much noise mutilating the dead whale. A comic genius, Stubb. The Seinfeld of his time.

Now, two final small things:

First, I take it back; maybe Hemingway did read *Moby Dick*. At least he read to the second paragraph of chapter 66. For right there in five lines, Melville hands him the entire idea for *Old Man and the Sea*.

Secondly. In chapter 65 there is the telling of an instance of a group of Englishmen who were able to survive for months eating moldy scraps of whale blubber. This happened when they "were accidentally left in Greenland by a whaling vessel." Melville tells us no more than that. Weren't you a bit curious about this "accident?" What happened? A month or so after the ship left Greenland did someone say to the captain, "Hey, wait a minute. Has anyone seen Nigel, Simon and Cecil lately?" After which there was a lot of scratching of heads and finally it dawned on them that maybe they'd been left in Greenland with all that moldy whale blubber?

terry.

5-27-04 – Phoenix (Chapters 61-70)

Terry.

Finally a whale is spotted and killed and the dead whale is brought back to the boat. Ahab is depressed about the killing of this whale because it only reminds him that *Moby Dick* is still out there.

All it takes is one man to be passionate and untold numbers will follow his sick vengeful passion anywhere. Witness the battle of Troy in Homer. Witness the mad men who follow Al Qaeda's Ahab: Osama bin Laden.

Stubb calls the black cook Fleece over to him. He accuses Fleece of overcooking the whale steak, and tells him to go and preach to the sharks, who are devouring the whale lashed to the side of the ship, to stop eating so loudly. Fleece goes over to the side of the boat, and delivers a "sermon" for Stubb:

"'Your woraciousness, fellow-critters, I don't blame ye so much for; dat is natur, and can't be helped; but to gobern dat wicked natur, dat is de pint. You is sharks, sartin; but if you gobern de shark in you, why den you be angel; for all angel is not'ing more dan de shark well goberned.'"

Can you picture Denzel Washington playing this part? The hilarious moron-savant? The happy idiot, abused and made fun of by all because he is our black man on board? I can't picture it. Actually, the sermon is very funny. Telling the sharks, "If you govern the shark in you, you will be an angel." (I have taken the blackface out of the language.)

Cruelty is often not seen for what it is until later. Thank God we would not allow this today, although Spike Lee might want to make an angry movie that allowed it to be seen. There was cruelty on the playgrounds of my youth, and there was a particular bully whom I would not hesitate to assassinate right now if my government asked me to. And I am a peaceful man.

Fleece tells you to govern the shark in you, and you may become an angel. Chesterton said the only reason angels can fly is because they take themselves lightly. Well, I have lost 13 pounds now! I am lighter by 13. As I govern the whale in me. My inner whale. Living a sedentary life in cars, on planes and in front of my computer, I had become a beached whale. 225 pounds. More body fat than *Moby Dick* himself. A symbol of America's obesity epidemic. Until I began to "gobern da whale."

In his latest book, *The Spooky Art*, Norman Mailer writes, "Name any great novel that didn't weary you first time through. A great novel has a consciousness that is new to us. We have to become imbued with this new consciousness before we can enjoy the work." He cites *Moby Dick* as an example.

He also writes: "I happened to pick up *Moby Dick*. I hadn't thought about Melville ten times in the last thirty years, but as soon as I read the first page, I realized my later style was formed by Melville, shaped by his love of long, rolling sentences full of inversions and reverses and paradoxes and ironies and exclamation points and dashes."

When I read that incident of the accidentally-left-in-Greenland-Englishmen, I was struck by the fact that right there on a silver platter Melville had basically produced the scenario for *Home Alone*.

And then later, as they start eating whale blubber, that this was the foundation of the very first Atkins Diet.

You were right in your intimation that I was hiding my weight from you. I was ashamed to tell you my weight had gone up to 225.

I have now lost 12 pounds and am down to 213. My goal is 175. I will reach my goal.

Here is what I see as a major problem for people with weight-loss. I believe obese, excess weight is a result of instant-gratification-syndrome. I want to pleasure myself wherever and whenever I want. It's the shadow side of self-control. The inside out opposite and reverse of self-control. Just as alcohol is a form (illusory, in the end) of mood-control. Food is a form of pleasure control.

People want to be in control of what makes them happy. If they can't go to their theater seats with a huge sugary Coke and buttered popcorn and some Mason Dots then they are no longer in control. They are BEING controlled by some DIET. No way. I need to EAT to drown out the pain I feel about being so FAT.

That has to be turned around, and the brain has to be completely re-wired.

Pleasure, if you stay with it long enough, past the dis-couragement, past the plateaus, now starts to come in different ways. It comes from beating the system.

It comes from teaching yourself to have a 1400-calorie day and still enjoy the food and still feel as if you have had "enough."

But to get there you have to work backwards from the number. You have to be willing to play a game with yourself (or, to use harsher, more frightening language, to discipline yourself). You have to play as if you "have to" stay within the 1400. Just for that day.

It becomes a practice. Like learning to play a very difficult piece on the guitar.

If you have a concert coming up, you have to learn it. So you learn it.

It's the "have to" factor inside you that must be tapped in to at some point or other or else no breakthroughs. Just homeostasis, or worse.

It is no accident that you and I are reading a book about blubber and whaling at this time of ultimate weight loss in my life.

steve.

2 June 2004 – Barcelona

Steve,

You certainly have a point about the power of the monomaniacal. However, you cite only the evil examples. Is monomania necessarily a bad thing? Can't it also work positively? In fact, you teach pretty much that same point in your books: figure out what you want to do -- then pursue it single-mindedly. Nothing could be simpler.

Blessed are the monomaniacs for they have only one thing on their to-do list.

I'm sure that the basic principle can be applied to weight-loss. You tend to accomplish what you focus your attention on. But the further ingredient is persistence. You know the thing I hate about our weight battles? The total commonplaceness of it. The clicheness of it. Two guys – quasi-athletic, reasonably fit heartbreakers hit middle age and start putting on whale blubber. Then spend the next thirty years in desultory pursuit of a series of diets, which they alternately get fired up about and then discouraged with. It's the ordinariness of all that that depresses me.

My own weight is like a Dennis the Menace child. It needs constant watching or it goes off on its own and gets in trouble. When we came to Barcelona on April 30th, I was at 181 (down from 197 on New Year's Day). Here I have paid no attention to what I eat or drink; so I was certainly aware that I'd put on some weight though I knew no specifics.

Part of the problem is the necessity over here of having a 700-plus math SAT score to figure out your weight. I mean, the scale tells you your weight – but in kilograms. So you step on the scale and you weigh 84.3. How do you feel? Great? Disappointed? Afraid you've somehow contracted a virulent cancer that's eating your flesh like Melville's sharks feasting on the whale? You simply don't know until you do the math. 84.3 kg x 2.2 = 185.46 lbs.

But I'm still not certain that this is how much I weigh right now because at my age I need to wear glasses to see the scale. And since I don't know what my glasses weigh, I don't know what to subtract from what the scale tells me to get my actual weight. All I know is that the last time I weighed myself in the U.S. I was 181. So right now I figure my glasses must weigh about 8 pounds. This seems somehow unlikely. So perhaps I'll have to start watching what I eat (and drink) again.

To that end, I want to thank you for all of the articles and research findings that you've been sending me on weight loss/gain. I regret to inform you, however, that the one trumpeting a study purporting to prove that a vigorous thirty minutes of walking a day will keep the weight off *even without dieting* (by dieting I mean limiting calorie intake) is totally in error.

I cite my own experience. I walk 35 minutes at a fast clip (about 4.4 mph) almost every day. I've been doing this for at least twelve years. By the end of the year my count is usually just above 300 walking days, so it averages a bit under six times a week. And yet, as I said, without watching the calories like Mr. Wilson watched Dennis, the weight sneaks up.

So as much as I'd love the study to be valid, I have to announce it's bullshit. Closer examination would no doubt reveal the study was paid for by the Pedometer Manufacturers Association.

You present Mailer's opinions on *Moby Dick* neutrally. But are you starting to agree? Are you beginning to think that maybe there is something there? I still find it, more than anything, a very curious choice for The Great American Novel. But it sure do sprawl.

t.

6 June 2004 – Phoenix

terry.

I love Mailer. I thrill to him, even when he is 90% b.s. His writing just soars in so many unexpected ways that I can't help but love him. So if Melville spawned Mailer, as Mailer sort of claims, can I not now love Melville for that alone?

How old is Andrew? As we prepare for our trip to Nova Scotia to see your son get married, it occurs to me that he is Melville's age when M wrote *Moby Dick*. You and I? We are Ahab's age! I read the other day that Melville thought so much of Hawthorne that he considered himself to be Bobby Vee to Hawthorne's Buddy Holly.

It looks as if you may be right about Smarty Jones. His second in the Belmont Stakes yesterday may be the signal that he is just, as you said, a very good horse. I read one story that even went so far as to say that Birdstone would have won the Derby too had he not thrown a shoe.

Did you get to SEE the race? Are you in civilization? (Electronically speaking I mean. I know you are in the land of beauty where all the women are dark and seductive and all the men look like Antonio Banderas.)

I am down 15 pounds since I started my project. And I agree with you about the walking. People are now telling me that I look good enough and my quest to go to high school weight is foolish. Yet I am going there anyway. Because I said I would. And I have to say that of ALL the weight-loss things I've fanatically monomaniacally read in these past three months, nothing works better or is clearer than your own system. Which I am using a version of. I'm 15 pounds down with 35 to go.

s.

9 juny 2004 – Barcelona, Catalunya

steve.

No, I did not see the race. It wasn't carried over here, or at least nowhere we could discover. Horse racing is barely mentioned here. There is not a track in the vicinity of Barcelona, which seems odd to me. It is, after all the second city in Spain. It would be the equivalent of there not being a race track in Los Angeles. There is an important track in Madrid.

American sports in general have to be followed via internet or (with a two day delay) in the IHT (International Herald-Tribune). Part of the problem is time. When the Lakers were tipping off against the Pistons in the first game of the NBA finals on Sunday, it was 5 AM here. This is not big television viewing time.

You are technically correct in thinking that we are in Spain, but you would have a hard time convincing a lot of people here of that. For them, we are living in Catalunya. And while they aren't violent about this like the Basques, they are passionate.

We had dinner on Saturday with two couples (the host is the Catalan translator of Paul Auster [extremely popular in Europe] and John Irving) and Miranda brought up the question of Catalunyan independence, which we sometimes see promoted in local graffiti.

All four of them are young, in their mid-30s, and all four would vote for Catalunya to become an independent country if certain economic deals with Spain could be worked out. Marta, the hostess, spoke several times of "my country" in referring not to Spain, but to Catalunya. Their major fear, discussed again and again when we meet with people here is language. Though they all speak Spanish perfectly, they worry about losing Catalan. (Reminds me of Quebec and French.)

During dinner, by agreement and for our benefit, conversation was in either Spanish or English. At one point Marta and the other woman, Mene, started laughing and it was explained that the four of them all vaguely had the feeling that they were acting in a play because they were so unused to speaking to each other in Spanish. It's all very interesting to us, and something that we really didn't notice at all the other times we've been here for shorter stays of only a few days or a week.

Melville was only 32 when *Moby Dick* was published. Andrew was 34 on April 2nd. So yes, it is not just *Two Guys Read Moby Dick*. It's *Two* Old *Guys Read Moby Dick*. I must say that despite the evidence of the calendar and two young boys outside of Detroit that call me "grandfather," I don't feel that old yet and am always caught off guard when a ticket seller asks me if I want the senior rate. I know this is trite, an attitude I would cross out of a piece of fiction as too ordinary and boring to read about, but there you have it. For that is the ultimate demeaning thing that age does to us – it turns us into clichés.

We are so happy that you're making the trip to Nova Scotia for Andrew's wedding. I know it's a long haul for you, but it will be great to see you both. The last time was when you came to New York last year (it was last year, wasn't it?). According to our schedule we will have just finished the *Moby Dick* the week before and what better place to celebrate the end of our voyage than in a great sea-faring town like Halifax. Herman would have approved. We will toast Andrew, Melissa and Melville and sing whaling songs 'til dawn, much to the confusion of the other guests.

Terry.

10 June 2004 – Phoenix

terry.

I'm thinking we should hire a sound crew and do a live CD of you and me singing those whaling songs as a "companion piece" to the first 500,000 readers of our book. "Two Guys – Live From Halifax!"

You may rest assured that I certainly do not think of you as old. Nor do I see myself as Walter Brennan. I even think I look about 40! (Kathy says this is not true). I am younger than Nabokov was when he wrote ADA, and that's all I have to know, and all I have to say to anyone who wants to talk about how "old" I am. Nabokov was pissed to die in the middle of writing *The Original of Laura*. Updike includes an incredible VN short story in his collection of the best short stories of all time. Do you know GISH JEN? Young Chinese-American writer, *New Yorker*, etc. real name: Lilian Jen, changed it to Gish as a pen name. You probably already know all about her being more modern-lit hip … but she has a short story in there too and I was impressed.

Who are the Pistons by the way? I mean, I watched them play but I kept saying like Butch and Sundance, Who Are These Guys? William Goldman, *Boys and Girls Together*, now there's a pop writer!

love to M

s.

14 June 2004 – Barcelona (Chapters 71-80)

S.

We nail another whale, a Right whale this time. So isn't that what we're here for? No. In fact it seems almost beside the point – we're after the Big One. This ten-chapter-span also includes the usual grotesqueries like the Jeroboam's story, which seems more like Poe than Melville. Plus further cetology lessons, this time examining the suspended heads of the dead Sperm and Right whales.

And so the Pequod sails on but the book seems a bit in the doldrums. The tip off that Melville senses this is in the chapter where he talks about the Sperm whale's head as a potential battering ram. In case we're getting a bit bored by all this zoological detail about the whale, he tells us to be sure and remember this when other (presumably more exciting) things happen.

I must admit though, that I did get a little thrill at the mention of Michigan in the last paragraph of chapter 74. For me, it was the decade's (in the sense of ten chapters) highlight. It was an insignificant mention, but still, there it was – Michigan! – state of our childhoods. Water Wonderland. State of Wolverines and Spartans. Of Lions and Tigers and Red Wings and Pistons. "If you seek a pleasant peninsula, look about you." State of real winters and the U.P. State of great forests and the Great Lakes. State of mind. It just lightened my day to know that even in 1851, Melville was aware of us, though he probably could not have anticipated the Hunter-Maple Pharmacy, Cunningham's or even the mighty Maples.

[These last three mentions are all references to our shared boyhoods in Birmingham, Michigan. The first two were hangouts for us at major crossroads in 1950-60s Birmingham, while

"Maples" was the nickname of the Birmingham Seaholm High School sports teams. TNH]

So we're in a bit of a lull, but – is it just me? – do there seem to be the beginnings of a skew toward the philosophical? Is Melville becoming more reflective at this point in the book? First there is the conversation between Flask and my man Stubb about the devil's being on the Pequod. This is the conversation that ends with Flask asking: "Now do you mean what you say and have been saying all along, Stubb?" And Stubb answering, "Mean or not mean, here we are at the ship."

Ah, the enigmatic Stubb! A line worthy of opening a Hamlet soliloquy. To my way of thinking, the man has been much underrated and unnoticed in the last century's worth of *Moby Dick* criticism. For me he is the true spiritual center of the novel.

Melville follows this with his warning for man not to read Kant, Locke and presumably other philosophers ("thunderheads" he calls them). The reward for giving up these wooly-headed intellectual know-it-alls is that "then you will float light and right." But he is not above a little sermonizing himself when, just a few lines later, he tells us not to "enlarge" our mind, but subtilize it.

I very much go along with him on this last. And though I've probably never said it aloud in exactly that way, it's a desire that has been growing on me these last few years. I want to spend the rest of my life developing a deeper mind, not a broader one. Of course this opens me up to all the possibilities of becoming pretentious but I promise you, Steve, I will resist this temptation with all my strength.

It's simply that I more admire the mind that can discern and dissect the nuance in our daily lives than the man who can explain the big bangs of the universe. I do not find this burrowing-down a second-rate occupation. I think it much more fascinating than, say, black holes, just to pick an example everyone can relate to. I know it's very fashionable nowadays to have a black hole expert at your cocktail party, but to be honest, they leave me cold. And while the rest of the party is enthralled for hours by the intricacies, oddities and meanings of various, popular black holes, I am off in a corner reading a book. I mean what are the odds I'm ever going to come up against a black hole in the day to day? 75-1? 80-1?

To end this, I must give Melville credit for a small but fine moment when he foreshadows the advent of Paris Hilton and other unexplainable, party-going celebrities of our time with: "Has the Sperm Whale ever written a book, spoken a speech? No, his great genius is declared in his doing nothing in particular to prove it."

t.

15 June 2004 – Phoenix (Chapters 71-80)

terry.

Melville should have called this *The Whales and the Males* as these men sail to the sea to find metaphors for understanding what they are running from (relationships with women and children?). Ishmael is a dreamer of the day, ruminating on all aspects of the slaughtered and showcased whales' heads. What does all of this suggest about mankind?

What is this evil being chased so dramatically in this book? If Ahab is psychotic in his revenge, and Fedallah is a kind of dark shadow of him, dimensionalizing his evil, an H.P. Lovecraft kind of one-dimensional Merlin, then who on this ship is real? Stubb, your favorite, seems to personify humor and fun (although he has his cruel streak, too.) But the question I cannot seem to answer for myself is Why? Why are all these men following this madman on this mission?

One might as well ask why the people around Bush follow him to Iraq, or the people around Johnson follow him to Viet Nam or the people around Nixon follow him into the Watergate complex. Why?

I believe Melville's answer is that these men are swept up on the waves of metaphor. Seduced by symbols. Like, in poetry, Amy Lowell and the imagists. Swept up in a sea of simile, scooped out of the slaughtered whale's head.

However, I constantly call Freud to mind as I read on. He said – admitted, really – that sometimes a cigar is just a cigar. So I want to urge someone on the ship, Ishmael? (no, too late! he is too smitten with the sexy savage Queequeg!), Starbuck, maybe, urge Starbuck to wake up and realize that nothing on this voyage means anything. Not really. Ahab is looking for hate in all the wrong places.

Why is this book such a classic? Intimidation. Melville intimidated the critics with the sheer force of his intellect and the wild scope of his writing, driving so deep into whaling lore and anatomical detail. Like Mailer's *Of a Fire on the Moon*, he is relentless: Journey to the Center of the Subject.

But, again, I can't help but see them as diving deep into symbol so as to escape a life, a whole life, that other great writers have not tried to escape. Some think if your escape is noisy enough, you'll be celebrated and they won't notice that you ran. So ... embarrassed as I am to say this, I really am not enjoying this book!

Steve.

16 Junio 2004 – Barcelona

Steve.

I must say that in one sense I very much understand your non-enjoyment of the book. Because, in truth, my enjoyment is coming largely in examining an artifact – a Great American artifact. I like pawing over it and wondering at what made this ... curiosity (I can think of no better word to describe it) the "G.A.N." Your suggestion that it was Melville's intellectual bullying that made the critics fall in line would carry more weight with me if the book had been a critical success while he was alive. But it wasn't. In fact it was more than 50 years after its publication that it began gaining the bulk of its reputation. But is it a joy to read? Do I look forward to reading each new chapter? Is it a page-turner? Well I think you've already answered these questions.

All of which surprises me, because the other candidate for the "GAN," *Huckleberry Finn*, is a wonderfully fun book to read. Very funny: very enjoyable.

With *Moby Dick*, I keep feeling that I'm missing something. That those critics must see something I don't. And one of the things I may be missing is the historical critical context. I mean, certainly there was a time at the beginning of the last century and through World War I when the forever-insecure United States was looking for validation of its national identity in all aspects of the relatively young country's life. It was a time when we were beginning to flex our muscles industrially and militarily, so what about in literature?

Who were we, literarily? All of which leads me to the suspicion that the concept of the "Great American Novel" came prior to the search for it. You know, the then-current literary types sat around and said – okay, if we are really a vital nation with our own cultural identity, then we should be able to point to a uniquely American literature, so what is the quintessentially American novel? Thus was born the concept of the GAN. It wasn't until they had the concept that they started looking for the novel to wear the clothes.

And they sort of backed into it. In the first place, there weren't that many serious candidates. Hawthorne (who Melville, that jock-sniffer, would have voted for) has a couple of problems. In the first place Hawthorne always characterized himself as a writer of "romances," which he did not think of as a pejorative term. But how could we name as our quintessential American writer a spinner of romances? The second problem was that his subject matter was not uniquely American.

James Fenimore Cooper? Yes, he wrote about the frontier, a concept that is essential to us, but, God, the prose! If you think Melville lacks brilliance as a stylist, put him next to Cooper and you'll think he's Shakespeare.

So that left Melville and Twain. Melville wrote about the masculine, courageous all-American enterprise of whaling and Twain wrote (at least in *Huck Finn*) about the frontier and the essence of humanity in a nation of slave-holders – both big themes and both very American.

Personally, I think the better candidates would have been Ralph Waldo Emerson and Walt Whitman. Unfortunately neither of them wrote novels. (The other problem with Emerson as far as I'm concerned is that I find him a Z-factory. I know you're a fan, but I don't think there are more than a handful of his sentences that I haven't fallen asleep in the middle of.)

As evidence of the validity of my theory of the way the GAN concept came about, I would cite the fact that the concept of the Great *English* Novel doesn't exist. There are definitely "Great Novels" and "English Novels," but they'd think you rather silly if you asked what they thought was the Great English Novel. Likewise, no such thing as the Great French Novel or the Great Spanish Novel. There's no need for those concepts in those countries – they know who they are. Whereas we still had to define ourselves. Well, now we have, and I guess we're whalers.

Your question about why all these guys are following madman Ahab on this mission is a good one. A short time out of port on a two- or three-year quest for whale oil and financial reward, but a Knute Rockne speech by Ahab and suddenly they don't seem to care about anything except catching *Moby Dick*. Yes, they've killed two whales since they've been out but it seems more like target practice rather than the goal of the whole enterprise. I can't answer the why on that one, but I've another for you: What kind of name is Ahab?

Doesn't it sound Arabic? (Wasn't there even a song called "Ahab the Arab.") Is he a Bin Laden precursor? A monomaniacal madman bent on destroying everything white and willing to commit suicide and take his followers with him in the execution of his mission.

t.

17 june 2004 – phoenix

terry.

Speaking of Melville's bullying, I didn't mean it in the social sense. I mean bullying within the pages. Like Mailer in much of his work, he keeps daring the reader to keep up with him, it's a violent spew of writing, showing off his intellect throughout, posing here as a humorist, and there as a journalist, now a biologist, now a philosopher. But it's a mess. Like the critics with Thomas Pynchon, intimidation occurs when they don't know what to make of a book BUT they recognize that they themselves could not have written it and they don't want to look stupid. It's like what Roger Ebert does with every single mediocre Spike Lee movie. He is so totally intimidated by Spike's angry authenticity (versus beached whale fat Roger the total bleached white intellectual fraud) that he fears looking stupid. We can trace a whole host of ills in our country to a fear of looking stupid. Melville's kowtowing critics, and the people who decide what high school and college kids must read foremost among them.

I agree with you on Emerson and Whitman and Twain. Especially on *Huckleberry Finn*'s being an enjoyable book to read. In my view, enjoyment would be the primary factor in the voting standards for the GAN. It would have to meet that criterion first. All else is pretense. Novels are entertainment first. Art second. They can be great art, like Nabokov's *The Gift*, but they must entertain all along the way or else they are tortured pretense. Or anger. Or, in Melville's case, the author doing therapy on himself.

Joyce Carol Oates, about whom John Updike has said, "If the phrase 'woman of letters' existed, she would be, foremost in this country, entitled to it," has likened *Moby Dick* and Melville's huge bouts of psychotic ebullience in writing it, to Jack Kerouac's booze-and-amphetamine fueled *On the Road* written, as we all know, on a single taped-together sheet of Chinese art paper that formed a prodigious and insane 150-foot roll that went through Kerouac's manual typewriter. I think that's a better comparison than to the wonderful *Huck Finn*. Is there anything wonderful in MD? There is nothing wonderful in it. There are admirable passages, and awesome stretches of very muscular writing, and there is great research and detail done on whaling, all admirable. But I've never liked a good symbol. Symbols are for those who can't write and who aren't happy enough to just tell it like it really is. Symbols for the novelist are like puns for the humorist.

Steve.

20 june 2004 – Barcelona

Steve.

I must say I agree with your distrust of symbols. People who cozy up to symbols are the same kinds of people who believe in reincarnation or Freud or Jung or, for that matter, the existence of God, or other unsubstantiated theories. I suppose it's comforting at some level, but I find it all so make-believe.

Symbols are, of course, members of the metaphor family. And when you use any metaphor you are lying. He was not literally a "tiger" when he came out for the fifth round (or a "Hurricane"). You have borrowed the tiger and his rightful properties to try to give an impression of what he was like in the ring. But, of course, it is a lie. You can argue that it is a lie to get to an essential truth, but you cannot, in the end, deny the lie.

We all use metaphors in our writing partly because they're useful, partly because they're fun, partly because they have become such a standard convention that they're hard to get away from; but mainly because writing itself is a lie. I mean this in the sense that all writing is one man's impression of something and is therefore untrustworthy.

In art, Magritte makes this same point with his famous painting of a pipe, one of those old-fashioned Sherlock Holmes type pipes, with the words "*Ce n'est pas un pipe*" ("This is not a pipe.") under it. Well, of course, it's not a pipe: it's a piece of canvas with oil paint on it. The oil paint is arranged in a way to remind you of what a pipe looks like, but the painting itself is certainly not a pipe. So, if you're an artist, and this strikes you like a thunderbolt of truth (now here I must caution you that I do not literally mean like a thunderbolt because this would probably kill you) then what do you do? Well, you invent abstract painting, which is all (and only) about paint on a canvas. Jackson Pollack did not create representations of anything. He created canvases with various kinds and colors of paint on them.

This same basic concept is expressed in literature by Gertrude Stein in "a rose is a rose is a rose." Now in my opinion, Gertrude is one of the leading producers of happy horseshit in all of the twentieth century, but who can argue with her on that one? A rose is not beauty; it is not love; it is not even Princess Diana – it is a rose. In other words: don't give me any metaphors, just call a spade and spade.

Anyway, if you are a writer and you are struck by this same thunderbolt (note earlier caveat) what do you do about it? Well, there's the example of John O'Hara who claimed at one point that he never used a simile or a metaphor in his writing for the very reason I raised of their unreliability. There were a couple of years in my twenties during which I read at least ten O'Hara books – novels, short stories and essays – and I don't think I knew about his claim at the time so I wasn't looking to see if he was as good as his word. But frankly I doubt if he was able to do what he said. Metaphors are too convenient a short hand, too ingrained in our language to avoid altogether. And who would want to?

Then there were the imagists. You've mentioned them several times in this correspondence usually citing Amy Lowell who I must admit to being not all that familiar with. I'm more familiar with the imagist poems of William Carlos Williams (e.g. "The Red Wheelbarrow") and Ezra Pound (e.g. "In a Station of the Metro" or something like that). But the basic theory behind the imagist poem was that an image, all by itself, without the writer adding any emotional content – just the plain, flatly-stated image – contains and communicates meaning.

In fact, I think that's true. But it seems to me there are problems with this as a sustainable form of literature. The first problem is that the image probably communicates a different meaning to every person who reads it. The second problem is if as a writer you're just going to lay it out there like a photograph for people to make of it what they will, then what is the role of the writer? It's a wonderful theory, but, like communism, who wants to live with the reality. The truth is they got bored with writing imagist poems pretty quickly. Didn't the Imagist movement only last about six or eight years? And even while they were writing them they cheated. For instance, in "The Red Wheelbarrow," it is the opening four-word stanza ("so much depends / upon") that really makes the poem, in my view. And what is that but WCW imposing his personal value hierarchy on the image?

By the way, if you took all the metaphor-haters I just mentioned and put them in one room, I don't think I'd much like to walk through the door. You've got that well-known drunk and professional boor O'Hara; the pompous, pontificating and thoroughly unreadable Gertrude; and the Nazi Pound. Williams is really the only one who sounds as if he might be pleasant to talk to.

Obviously I've rambled on about this too long and in a fairly helter-skelter manner so you aren't even sure what my overall point is. It therefore becomes necessary for me to summarize: 1) All metaphors are untrustworthy and potentially dangerous. 2) But because they are useful and rather fun, we will continue to encounter them. 3) They should, however, be approached cautiously.

And while all of this is true of metaphors in general, symbols – as the most extreme form of metaphor – are much the most dangerous. This is aggravated by the fact that symbols are usually pressed into service for the purpose of sermonizing or forwarding a specific philosophical point of view. This is always tedious. Further, symbols don't announce themselves; they leave the job of figuring out the meaning of the symbol to the reader. This is the source of much abuse and an absurd number of doctoral theses.

This all came to mind because yesterday I finally read the Introduction to *Moby Dick* from my travel copy of the book (Signet Classic). Usually I make a point of not reading introductions until after I've finished the book because sometimes an introduction will prejudice my reading, and I'd much rather develop my own prejudices. But I have been so baffled by the GAN status of the book that I wanted to read a bit on how this came about.

The Introduction is written by a woman named Elizabeth Renker who teaches English at Ohio State (immediately making her suspect in my book – I'll bet she's one of the professors who gave Maurice Clarett a passing grade to keep him eligible for football).

Anyway, in case you were wondering about the symbolism in the book, let me throw this quote into your thinking process:

"Scholars have suggested that the Pequod *is in fact the American ship of state, careening toward civil war, fueled by the labor of people of color (such as Ahab's harpooners), and finally destroyed by its fixation on whiteness."*

Give me a break! But if Melville did intend that symbolic reading, then I suggest he should drop out of the running for a "great writer" title for the overall benefit of literature. In fact, he should think twice before applying for "good writer."

terry.

29 June 2004 – Barcelona (Chapters 81-90)

Steve.

The above date is correct in terms of when I am writing this, but I'll probably not be able to send it off to you until the first of July because we're basically flying all day tomorrow. After two months here we return to New York. This really is a quite remarkable city and even though I'd been here three or four times before, it was very full of great surprises.

Barcelona's effect on my various disciplines? Mixed.

I hate to bring up weight, because, as I said before, I feel such a cliché for writing about it, but the record here is fairly dreadful. Too many temptations. Wonderful and different foods, and the tapas style of eating is a killer. Still hungry? We'll take a little more of that and a little of this. Also the Catalunyans tend to eat their major meal at 2:30 or 3 in the afternoon. I was happy to go along with them on this, but then I'd add another major meal in the evening. All of this adds up to this bottom line: I think I put on four and a half to five kilos while I've been here. That's 10-11 pounds to you and, frankly, to me too starting July 1st, which coincidentally is the day I start my new diet.

On the other hand, today marks the 56th straight day that I've spent at least one hour writing. This is a record for me by at least 35 days. I had originally set out to try for 50 days. When I passed that mark last week I just kept it going. I'm rather pleased with myself I must say and I'd be tempted to go out and celebrate if it weren't for the fact that I have a hard time fitting through doors now.

(I wrote a play while I was here, by the way, which seemed to me a slightly less transparent way of meeting beautiful young actresses than writing a screenplay. Of course, it hasn't worked yet either. Anyway, the drawback of this achievement for you is that I will force you to read it.)

Yes, I've been avoiding *Moby Dick* so far in this letter, because frankly what's to say that we haven't already said. This decade of chapters features more zoology lessons, more whale legends – but, hang on there! – this time he sprinkles in a little history of whaling in the courts of law. But even in this slow-moving set of ten (has the plot progressed one bit here?) Stubb comes forward to save the day for me with his sarcastic exhortations to his rowing crew to pick up the pace: "We're becalmed! Halloo, here's grass growing on the boat's bottom."

Another strange thing for me is that I'm currently also reading Yann Martel's *Life of Pi*. And because they are both tales of men against the sea and the world of animals, I keep having to think twice about which book contains some passage or thought I wanted to comment on to you. In case you don't know, the *Life of Pi* is about a boy who is cast adrift on the ocean in a lifeboat with a tiger. This is almost exactly the kind of plot summary that makes me vow never to read the book. However, I had, not just one – but two, friends recommend the book. One said it was the best book he had read in years and he reads a lot. The second recommendation was almost as effusive. So I gave in. Well now I'm halfway through and I think my first inclination was correct. It's just a little too New-Agey for me. It does have a world of information about the animal kingdom in it, however, and you know how excited that makes me.

We're more that two-thirds of the way through *Moby Dick*! The end, if not quite in sight, is just over the horizon.

t.

3 July 2004 – New York again

s.

You quote Nietsche. Is that Ray Nietsche who used to play for Lombardi during the Golden-Era Packers? Or a different one?

I think you and I should book ourselves on one of those California whale-spotting cruises. But we should have made careful preparations beforehand so that when the whales are sighted, four or five fierce-looking, tattooed stowaways of indeterminate nationality burst from the men's room where they've been hiding and join us in lowering a boat. (I'm not sure of all the details of having the boat at hand, but I *am* sure that after all the instructions we've received from Melville we are fully capable of taking it from there.)

We'll go in full pursuit of Willie and put on a real show for all those left on the cruise watching on. And when the sea is red with whale gore and the Greenpeace people are screaming for a lynching, we'll maintain that we are merely upholding the great American whaling tradition. Plus I think we can legitimately claim that we are trying to lessen the country's dependence on Arab oil.

t.

16 July 2004 – New York (Chapters 91-100)

Steve.

Any lingering doubt about Melville's sexual proclivities was resolved for me in chapter 94 as Ishmael describes the squeezing of the sperm whale globules. Rather than impose my interpretation on you, I think I'll just quote:

"I found myself unwittingly squeezing my co-workers hands, mistaking their hands for the gentle globules. Such an abounding, affectionate, friendly, loving feeling did this avocation beget; that at last I was continually squeezing their hands, and looking up into their eyes sentimentally."

I think I told you earlier that when we started this project I had never heard anything about Melville's homosexual leanings. In fact, I tended to dismiss the suggestion as so much revisionist muck-raking. After reading the above passage, however, I must say that if you gave me a jury of twelve reasonable people, I'm pretty sure we could expect a unanimous verdict.

I must say I liked the sequence in chapter 96 where Ishmael literally falls asleep at the wheel. Then, of course, he ends it with "a lesson": "Never dream with thy hand on the helm! Turn not thy back to the compass."

Since reading this I have been living by these words and intend to do so for the rest of my days.

My love affair with Melville (Please note I use the term "love affair" in a purely figurative sense.) hit a very rocky patch when I got a glimpse of his difficulty with arithmetic. In chapter 99, "The Doubloon," he figures the coin is worth 16 dollars. A cigar costs 2 cents. So he figures that the doubloon is worth 960 cigars.

Is it true that Melville got the lowest math score in the history of the SATs?

But all of this is basically marking time, is it not? And for another ten chapters we get whaling lessons and virtually no story. Nothing happens! Suddenly, chapter 100! We meet another ship – the English ship the Samuel Enderby – that has actually encountered Moby Dick. They even report where the white whale is headed. Ahab gets over-excited and the chase is on. Is it possible that the final fifth of the book might actually turn into the adventure story we had anticipated going in?

When I write about the next ten chapters at the end of July, you will be reading the words of a newly-minted 60-year-old man. I have no doubt you will detect a deeper wisdom, a previously unrevealed sagacity and sharper, more incisive insights throughout. Until then.

terry.

In a small fishing village outside of Phoenix, Arizona, July 16, 2004:

Dear Terry,

PIP PLOPPED IN SPINGLE SPANGLE SEA

Our whaling ship's small cabin boy, Pip: a frail "little Negro" who entertains the rest of the sailors with his dancing and tambourine, may have been the prototype for Bob Dylan's "Mr. Tambourine Man" and even Jerry Jeff Walker's "Mr. Bojangles" later made so popular by Sammy Davis, Jr., whom I think of as looking exactly like Pip, Melville's frail "little negro."

When one of the ship's regular crew sprains his hand, Pip, our little tambourine man, is asked to take his place in the whale boat. This turns out to be a disaster: during his first outing in pursuit of a whale, the inexperienced Pip accidentally falls from the boat, becomes tangled up in a blue harpoon line and is nearly strangled to death. He is saved only by cutting the line, and thereby losing the harpooned whale, and the rest of the men are furious and think him an idiot. Stubb (your favorite funny man) tells Pip that if he goes overboard again, he will not be rescued. "But we are all in the hands of the Gods," Ishmael writes, and Pip falls in once again. "Alas, Stubb was but too true to his word," and the boat leaves Pip in the "spangled sea, calm and cool, and flatly stretching away, all round, to the horizon."

Pip is left in Melville's "spangled sea" (and yes, as we can all see, Melville was, in flashes throughout this massive compost of a book, a powerful poetic novelist.) The "spangled sea" reminds me of how Dylan's own tambourine man was left in the "jingle jangle morning" to come following me. These two wild writers finding a nexus at the jangle and the spangle.

Pip is left in the "awful lonesomeness" of the great ocean, abandoned by all the boats at once. He is eventually rescued "by the merest chance" when the ship passes by, but from that moment on, Pip becomes an "idiot." (Perhaps, but maybe I'm stretching, foreshadowing Dylan's great song, "Idiot Wind.")

As Ishmael put it, "the sea had jeeringly kept his finite body up, but drowned the infinite of his soul." The body of Pip here, I believe is what is described by Jerry Jeff Walker as the "dog" of Mr. Bojangles: ("He danced for those at minstrel shows and county fairs throughout the south/ He spoke with tears of fifteen years how his dog and he traveled about/ His dog up and died, up and died/ After twenty years he still grieved.") "Mr. Bojangles" was recorded by everyone from John Denver to Nina Simone, and it is forever poignant and hauntingly filled with a waltz beat and trance-inducing internal rhyme.

So Pip is left to drown, and if we were doing the movie today we would have Dylan's "Mr. Tambourine Man," perhaps by the Byrds, swelling up in the soundtrack as this tiny black man bobbed on the ocean, "Yes, to dance beneath the diamond sky with one hand waving free/ Silhouetted by the sea/ circled by the circus sands/ With all memory and fate/ driven deep beneath the waves/ Let me forget about today until tomorrow."

s.

17 july 2004 – New York

steve.

All things come together, of course. It has something to do with the spinning of the universe I think. But it also has to do with heightened awareness. In other words, all of these *Moby Dick* sightings that we've experienced in the last six months might well have gone unremarked were it not for the fact of our reading of the book.

With that, I report another:

Yesterday Miranda and I went to see *Before Sunset* with Julia Delpy and Ethan Hawke. It is the nine-years-after sequel to *Before Sunrise*. I assume you know the story because quite a bit has been written about it since the sequel came out, but the first movie ends with the two of them – after meeting on a train, spending one night together in Vienna and falling in love, parting – but agreeing to meet in Vienna again in six months. They don't meet. But nine years later, he has written a successful novel based entirely on that one night. He is in Paris doing a reading at Shakespeare and Company. She comes to the reading and the next hour and a half is the movie.

Embarrassingly I very much liked the movie, which along with its predecessor is hopelessly romantic. The movie is also very talky, but all the time they're talking they're walking through a part of Paris that was our home for three years so that was certainly part of why I liked it. I bring the whole thing up, however, not to expose my romantic side to you, but rather because at one point in the movie Julie is saying how great it is that he has written this bestseller and he dismisses it by saying, "Well, yeah, but most people haven't even read *Moby Dick*." She acknowledges that she hasn't herself. And yet in another two months we *will* have, though I'm sure we will both continue to be baffled by its reputation.

There were also a couple of other things in the movie that clicked with your letter of the 16th, which I had just read before going to the movie. 1) You mentioned the waltz beat in Bojangles and, in the movie, Julie sings the Ethan character a waltz song of her own composition. 2) Your mention of Nina Simone is also echoed in the film when Julie ends the film with about a two-minute Nina Simone imitation.

For reasons that will become clear when I send you my play, I have been spending a lot of time lately studying Hamlet. And just last week I read Harold Bloom's recent *Hamlet: Poem Unlimited*.

In chapter 1 Bloom announces that the greatest works in western literature are: the *Iliad*, the *Aeneid*, *The Divine Comedy*, *The Canterbury Tales*, *Hamlet*, *King Lear*, *Macbeth*, *Don Quixote*, *Paradise Lost*, *War and Peace*, *The Brothers Karamazov*, *Leaves of Grass*, *Moby Dick* and *Remembrance of Things Past*.

So there it is again.

t.

2 August 2004 – Phoenix

terry.

Ahab doesn't care that oil is spilling and that the ship's owners will lose their profits without it; he cares only about his obsessive pursuit of the whale. Starbuck is outraged, and won't return to the deck, even as Ahab threatens him with a gun, and declares "there is one God that is Lord over the earth, and one Captain that is lord over the *Pequod*." Starbuck retorts that Ahab should not fear Starbuck, but "let Ahab beware of Ahab; beware of thyself, old man." Ahab silently admits that Starbuck has a point, and announces that the ship will stop. It is a temporary return to sanity for Ahab.

I used to admire obsession. If a book came out called *The Magnificent Obsession*, I was in admiration of the concept even before I read the book. I used to believe that I myself needed more obsession in my life.

But Ahab illustrates the dead end nature of obsession. In an ugly, clumsy way, Melville has made this obsessed old man and the innocent whale he pursues a grotesquely convincing picture of obsession. A cautionary tale. Inside the shipwreck that is his book.

Hinckley's obsession with Jodie Foster led him to shoot President Reagan. An obsessed person stalks a phantom in the name of fulfillment or realization. "Only this will make me whole and complete," believes the obsessed person. It is an illusion.

Of course. And madness, as Melville shows us with Ahab. What I as a reader have been looking for is the opposite man on deck. The person who, rather than being obsessed with dark achievement and the pursuit of goals and objectives, is living in the moment, happy to be human. I believe that that person is Queequeg. Queequeg catches a fever and believes he is dying and asks that a canoe be made to carry him to his death. After he fasts and lies still for days Pip comes to him, the mad dancing bojangles little Pip, comes to Queequeg in the jingle jangle morning and babbles some divine gibberish and Queequeg's fever lifts. Queequeg says he "decided" not to die. Queequeg decided to think to himself, as if he were Dylan Thomas, "and death shall have no dominion."

And so I believe that all obsession is a fear of death. In disguise. Because if you take the wild idea that "if I can't have this, I'll just die," which is the obsessive's inner programming, and if you turn that around, you get, "But if I DO achieve this, I will live eternally, I'll be immortal, I'll be happy forever." But the key word is not "happy" it's "forever." Obsession is an inverted, perverted attempt at *forever*.

What Queequeg feels deeply is that forever is here and now. Which is why he is my hero in this book. He will take his inspiration from anyone and anything because he is *not* obsessed, he is receptive and open to life. So Pip's scat singing is as spiritual to him as a ponderous tablet from a mountain top.

When we were kids we always wanted to "be" someone in a movie or a book. "I'll be Gawain, you be Lancelot!" Through this book I've been secretly wondering who to be. Now I know. I'll be the cannibal Queequeg.

Steve.

5 August 2004 -- New York

S.

I apologize for my lateness in holding up my end. I have been very busy turning sixty. Even believing that I carried it off with some grace, I am not happy about it. The Bible gives you three score and ten and I figure modern medicine should be worth another ten. So at 60 I am entering the fourth quarter and I feel I am down by two touchdowns.

By this last I mean I feel I have wasted much of the first three quarters and will have to fight like crazy to put together a couple of TD drives. To this end – and to your discussion of obsession – I wish for *more* obsession in my life. I feel I am too balanced, too rational, too cautious, too un-headlong – and always have been. It is the obsessed that accomplish and build things; it is the rational who measure them.

Still, my rational override would have to agree with you and Melville that obsession is madness. It's just that at 60 I feel I may need a little madness to get those two touchdowns. On the other hand it is in my nature *not* to be obsessed. So I wonder if I can fake it enough to hit my wide receiver with the home run ball.

(Just to make sure I extend this metaphor beyond the breaking point, let me tell you that if I do manage to get that second touchdown just before I turn 80, I intend to go for one on the extra point. A tie, you see, would mean that I get to go into overtime. In this game winning isn't everything; playing is everything.)

Before we leave the subject, what does Calvin Klein have to do with obsession – I mean how much sense does that name make?

Thanks, by the way, for the birthday greetings – both your e-mail and the phone call. As you know, we were visiting Chicago and Wisconsin during the week leading up to my birthday. The first for fun. The second as part of my mission for you: to find in my brother's garage the file containing your correspondence with my father 1978-1988. But we are back in NYC for a while until we head off for Andrew's wedding in Halifax when we will see you and Kathy and sing a night's worth of whaling songs in celebration of our finally getting the *Moby Dick* monkey off our backs. And yes, we can also celebrate me finding the files.

[Steve knew my father from the time we were kids together in Birmingham, Michigan, until my father's death in 1988. Sometime in the early 70s, they became good friends and corresponded on a regular basis. It was actually my father as a former drunk who helped convince Steve to go to AA and to quit drinking. In doing so, he was merely repaying a favor to Steve, who had been instrumental in getting my father's first two books published. Several years ago, Steve decided he wanted to write a book about his relationship with my father and asked if he could get copies of their correspondence. After many months and years of trying to figure out whether the letters still existed or not, I managed to narrow the question down to a bunch of boxes of papers in my brother Tony's garage in Stoughton, Wisconsin. I promised Steve that on my next visit to Tony's I would go through all of the boxes to try to find the letters. Obviously I found them. TNH.]

I have a question. Early on in the book a great deal was made of Ahab's secret elite corps of whalemen who were kept out of sight until the first lowering. And yet, once they were out of the closet, what happened to them? We've basically heard nothing from this ghostly band of mutants since that one chase.

Doesn't that strike you as odd? Aren't you curious? Are we to assume this group has simply blended in with the rest of the crew, singing sea shanties and playing gin rummy and practical jokes with Stubb, Ishmael, Fleece, Pip and the rest? How likely does that seem? I don't cite this as an oversight on Melville's part, obviously he finds this phantom crew no longer literarily useful. But the whole thing raises an even bigger issue for me: if this crew was supposed to be some kind of symbol, then of what? Further, if the whole book is a parable, then a parable of what? Here we are 5/6s of the way through the book and I am no closer to answering those questions than I was when we started this book.

This whole issue lends credence to your theory of Melville brow-beating the intellectual critics with ambiguity and opacity. ("If I can't understand it then it must be profound and great." It is this measure, of course, that would make *Finnegan's Wake* the greatest book in the English language – or whatever language it is in.)

What does an author owe a reader? How impenetrable is he allowed to be before an arrest can be made and prosecution through the criminal courts can commence? In truth I think this novel is a bit of a mess. Each chapter seems fine on its own, meaning that when you read any single chapter you come away with an impression of what the book is going to be like. However, your impression, based on that one chapter, would always be wrong. Each chapter feels as if it's part of another book. And it's not just *one* other book, it's many – and quite a few of them aren't even fiction.

As I reach the end of the book I realize that, while I am enjoying the process of reading the book and thinking and writing about it, I am not much liking the actual book itself. If this is the "great American novel," then I'm pretty sure I can beat it. Yes, I know, it's time I put some hard cash in my mouth.

Still … every once in a while I come upon something in the book that I quite enjoy. Something that amuses me or makes me think. You know I like Stubb, and I certainly admire Starbuck and your cynosure Queequeg for their steadfastness and "skill sets" (as they'd be called now). And occasionally Melville will write something that takes me by the hand down a thought-path for a bit. But in the end, they're just fragments.

Perhaps the book is best thought of as a collection of fragments, as a collage. I say collage rather than mosaic because a mosaic implies some discernible pattern, all the pieces coming together as a recognizable image when one stands back and looks at it. And while a collage is also individual fragments put together to form something new, the organizing principle is rarely as clearly defined, in fact it is sometimes patently and purposely obscured or totally missing. Looked at in this light, *Moby Dick* becomes a harbinger of modernism, a trailblazer on a path that takes us to *Ulysses* and *The Waste Land*, which works both resemble the collage form.

I can imagine the lousy grade I would get if I tried out any of these fairly blunt ideas in a college, or even high-school, level course paper. And yet, they seem rather obvious to me. In fact – in spite of the hubris on display in saying this – I think both our comments on the book throughout this correspondence have been much more sensible and normal reactions than those of literary studies people.

Why is that?

I think that part of the answer is that our reactions and analysis do not desperately search for obscure points or attempt radical interpretations. People whose jobs and careers rely on writing about literature can't afford to state the obvious because if that was all they did then wouldn't people say "Hey, what do we need you for?" There is also the competitive nature of the academic arena that won't allow them to say something that all the other *Moby Dick* scholars are saying because if they did then wouldn't their universities say, "Hey, what do we need you for?" And there is also the point that we are willing to have fun in our reading of the book and don't treat it as some kind of sacred text that can only be approached with serious looks on our faces. Academics, of course can't afford to have any fun with it because if the book can be seen as enjoyable and not the reincarnation of some wrathful god then universities might just say, "Hey, what do we need you for?"

What I bemoan is their need to obfuscate and find obscure theories and explanations to succeed in their profession. Of course, to a certain extent this is forced on them by the academy so it's hard to blame them, but is it really necessary? I suppose so. And isn't it true that we all promote the difficulties and complexities of our work in order to exalt it and avoid being asked the question: "Hey, what do we need you for?"

What got me thinking about how critics treat literature and prompted me to spin off on this little tangent was that while I was looking in Tony's garage for your correspondence file, I came across a file of my father's English literature papers, written in 1970 and '71 when he was getting his Master's Degree. I read parts of several of them – one of which [the Malcolm Lowry piece], in a revised form, you published as part of Dad's book *Booze, Books and the Big Deuce*. Thankfully all these English papers seemed very sensible. I wonder how *he* would have fared in an academic community.

Anyway, amongst these papers fittingly was a seven-page essay on the Pequod's first mate Starbuck. I will bring it to Halifax. You'll enjoy reading it.

By the way, what's going on with your weight?

t.

7 August 2004 – Phoenix

Terry.

Okay, I'll buy this. This, in your case, is a good obsession because it's an over-correction. Like the Buddhists do, to get you to the most spiritual path, what some of them call the middle way, they pull you back all the way over to one side to over-correct and get you to come to the middle.

I will be in full support of your scoring two touchdowns in your final quarter (I hereby grant you life until you are 80 in order to do this. As long as you never and I mean NEVER stop writing. That would be the price.)

But then, to obey the metaphor, do not try to get it all back in one play. The best comebacks in the history of football worked because somehow in the midst of the amazing comeback the team that came back was patient enough to play one play at a time and not try to get it all back with some insane trick Hail-Mary play. Each day is another play.

You asked about my weight, noting my recent silence on the subject. I am living on a plateau. After losing 17 pounds, I have not lost another. Nor have I gained. Somehow I have found an amount of food I can take in during a week's time that keeps me where I am. In truth, the priority has slipped for me. Or, as Dr. Phil would say, "I took it off project status."

Why did I do this? I think it was self-defense. I had three books I was writing at once, and needed to finish them all. One is finished and at the publisher for a November release. The other two are in progress. In addition, I was dealing with the emotion of having my final child move out of the house and away from home. I have been a single father with full custody of four children for many many years. And it had become a mother. Or, rather, I myself had become a mother.

Excuse Number Three: My seminar and travel schedule became insane. I have been in Canada twice, and in distant cities many times in the past two months. I have averaged four talks a week in the past two months, most of which are in odd, ugly cities. (Get me out of here!)

Yet I have somehow not gained weight. I'm skating the plateau like Brett Hull who was just traded to the Phoenix Coyotes.

S.

17 August 2004 – New York (Chapters 110-120)

Steve.

Perhaps it's merely that I'm not used to the 1850 style, but in reading *Moby Dick*, I often have a hard time figuring out what's going on. Literally. For instance, I had to read chapter 125 (I know this is outside my chapters 110-120 jurisdiction, but I just finished reading this chapter) several times before I was able to take a good calculated guess at what happened. I still haven't come close to working out the "why."

And this is not an isolated instance. I had similar difficulty working out the facts in the case of Perth, the blacksmith. Obviously he had some kind of problem that destroyed his whole life, but what was it? After several readings I have come to believe that the man had/has a drinking problem. Am I right? I mean the only real clue is the line: "It was the bottle conjurer." So I figure it's either a drinking problem or a magician who does tricks with bottles.

I find it interesting that in this instance Melville again presents the sea as the great escape. Perth – totally destroyed by his problems (whatever they may have been), his wife and children in their graves – escapes his past and the troubles of this world by going to sea. This is not the first time in the book Melville has offered the sea as the place to escape the cruel, workaday world. In fact, it's almost the first thought in the book when Ishmael says that whenever it is "a damp, drizzly November in my soul I count it high time to get to sea as soon as I can."

I've read a number of critics over the years who have said that one of the things that has most influenced America and American literature has been the concept of the frontier. That we could always move on. That whenever things got rough, or we were looking for new adventures and challenges, we could always "light out for the territories," in the famous *Huckleberry Finn* phrase. Melville seems to have made a frontier of the sea, which is why he seems so "American." Think of the novels coming out of Europe at about this time: Dickens, Thackeray, Trollope, Dumas, Hugo, Tolstoy, Dostoyevsky, Turgenev. However their novels stack up against Melville (and you wouldn't get a big argument out of me if you said they were better), not one of their books even remotely resembles *Moby Dick*. I'm not sure they could even have envisioned that a book could be written like that.

These ten chapters also confirmed my fondness for Stubb – not only the great humorist, but the great optimist too. As he himself says: "I am Stubb, and Stubb has his history, but here Stubb takes oaths that Stubb has always been jolly."

And here as Melville rains portent down on the Pequod, and the rest of the crew is making dire predictions with each new sign, Stubb is blithely optimistic, seeing each event as a positive sign. For example, as everyone is quaking with fear during the typhoon when St. Elmo's fire turns the ship into a fireworks display, Stubb says the eerie flames on the top of the masts signal great whale hunting and full oil barrels ahead.

I stand second to no man in my admiration for Stubb, but where has he been?! The ship is in the middle of the "perfect storm;" is in full pursuit of a whale that is famous for being deadly; and is in the control of a madman, whose madness is becoming more and more apparent every day. Someone should set Stubb's alarm clock.

Clear-eyed Starbuck, on the other hand, seems to be coming unhappily unto his own.

And hey, don't you love a good prophecy? The forewarning that seems on its face impossibly improbable and thus gives the unsuspecting victim a real sense of confidence.

Macbeth safe until Birnam Wood comes to Dunsinane.

Oedipus who will kill his father and marry his mother.

Caesar told to beware the Ides of March.

And now, Ahab who, before he can die, will see two hearses – the first not man-made, and the second made of American wood. And he is told only hemp can kill him.

He, of course, figures he's safe. Well, call me crazy, but I'm not so sure.

In closing, Steve, thanks for consenting to read my play, *Hamlet – The Sequel*. I really need someone to look at it besides me. As you know, it's the first play I've ever written and I'm flying blind. It's one of those things that you get into, somehow work your way through and in the end you have something that looks something like a play. Initially I'm just grateful for that. But now comes the question of whether it's halfway decent or not. And on that question I feel totally inadequate to put forward even the glimmer of an answer.

Terry.

18 August 2004 – Phoenix

terry.

So now all speculation about Ahab being crazy and demonic is no longer speculation as he gets really "out there," ordering a super-harpoon to be made and dipped in blood while chanting allegiance to the devil himself.

Does that make the whale the Christ? Is this book a watery crucifixion? The fact that I can even ask that question demonstrates how wild a mess this book has become. Here's something I suspect: Melville's just making this stuff up as he goes. I mean that's what a novelist always does anyway, right? But in this book it is right up into the reader's face that he's flying high with no flight plan. But if I admired William Burroughs and Jack Kerouac for their purposelessness, then why not Melville? Maybe it's because Melville's book stands as a great classic and students today are still forced to read it.

As Ahab was having his special harpoon dipped in blood and as he ranted his devil's homage, I began to think of how I would select the sound track for this book should it be made into a new movie. I couldn't get a certain bad old song out of my head because the song would be so perfect for these last chapters of Ahab's now vividly diabolical obsessed quest. The song was by a group called "The Crazy World of Arthur Brown." You remember how the record starts, with Arthur shouting "I am the god of hell fire!" The record was called "Fire" and it was a big hit in the late sixties. A truly awful record. Perfect for this book's final stages.

I did a little research on Arthur Brown, by the way, and I found to my surprise that he was a well-educated Englishman. However, he really got into his god of hell fire image and would come on stage in the late '60s with his hair on fire and end the song "Fire" completely nude. After being arrested for that in Italy, Brown, who was not in court, sent the magistrates an explanation saying his striptease dance was based on Viking rituals and symbolized the cleansing of the mind. I may have to do that same ritual after reading the last pages of this novel.

Brown has had a wild life! In 1991 Arthur Brown was admitted into The Church of Universal Life as a full-fledged Minister. This sounds pretty impressive, but when you learn that other "ministers" include Cary Grant and James Mason, I think we begin to get the picture.

Steve.

23 August 2004 – Phoenix (Chapters 120-135)

terry.

Captain Ahab foretold the whole story of *Moby Dick* when he said early in the novel, "It was that accursed white whale that made a poor pegging lubber of me forever and a day! I'll chase him 'round Good Hope, and 'round the Horn, and 'round perdition's flames before I give him up. And that is what ye have shipped for, men! To chase that white whale on both sides of land, and over all sides of earth, till he spouts black blood and rolls fin out."

Melville himself joked nervously that this was not a really finished book. It was "a draught of a draught" is what he admitted to. Its unfinished quality is what a sober reader would also see immediately. It's what I saw. In my imagining mind I also saw droves of people trying to be English majors in college bailing out once they were assigned this book and told it was "THE great American novel." If this was the great American novel why would you want to major in Literature? Fortunately the English I majored in also featured D.H. Lawrence, James Joyce, Thomas Hardy, E. M. Forster, and writers who could write a novel and not finish it until it was finished.

In the end of this book, the rope from Ahab's harpoon coiled about his neck and wrenched him from his quest. All the crew was lost with the ship, except for Ishmael, who found safety by clinging to Queequeg's floating coffin. (The musical would have him singing a Judy Garland song during this scene.) He alone was rescued to tell the tale of this ill-fated boat that "like Satan, would not sink to hell till she had dragged a living part of heaven along with her…" That living part of heaven was the infrequent poetic writing throughout by Melville.

Melville's heavy sea adventure is a book which sold fewer copies in Melville's life time than any one of the seven unheard-of books I have written in my own life time. I argue that the people in his lifetime knew a good book when they didn't see one. Instead of just putting a good sea adventure out there, Melville wanted to explore the archetypes of good and evil struggling together within the tenets of eighteenth-century Calvinism. It was that boring obsession that excited scholars who came along later and mistook this book for a "classic."

Scholars say that in all his books Melville wrestles with man's place in the cosmos, endeavoring to expose the unseen forces of the universe and the effects of these forces on man. By doing this, he repeatedly lets his readers down. Because readers don't suffer from those questions, unless they are hung over or insane. Some professors say that in *Moby Dick*, Melville recognizes the power of both God and the Devil, and strains to comprehend their invisible source. "Strains" is the key word here. He strains throughout, at our expense. And he strains to find answers to questions we don't care

about. That's the real problem. Questions of the hypocrisy of
Calvinism and the true nature of mythological religious
superheroes are simply not interesting. They are private and very
personal battles an angry Melville was wrestling with and scholars
mistook all this wrestling for brains. It was as wrong as mistaking
the World Wrestling Federation for a sport. Wrestling is wrestling.
That's all it is.

steve.

24 August 2004 – Saratoga, NY

Dear Steve,

I agree that no one cares about those issues like the hypocrisy
of Calvinism, etc. I rarely meet anyone at a cocktail party who even
brings up the name Calvin unless it is linked with Hobbes. But at
the same time I wonder if Melville's contemporaries *did* worry
about those issues. Could it be? They were obviously a rather dull
lot if they did.

You also say that the critics who sparked the Melville revival
fell in love with this issue of Good and Evil. That seems fine to me
if you go for that sort of thing which I, like you, don't. But my
question is who or what is Good and likewise, who or what is Evil
in the book. It's not all that clear to me. Is Ahab Evil and Moby
Dick Good? As I said earlier in these letters, if you're going to write
a book filled with symbols, at some point I think you owe it to the
reader to make it clear what the symbols are. Wouldn't you think?
I might also say that I always distrust a writer who says that he is
"wrestling with man's place in the cosmos." I want to read a novel
about man's place on Bleecker Street.

But it's over. At long last I have turned the final page of *Moby
Dick*. And a rather abrupt ending it was, didn't you think? After

drawing out so much along the way, suddenly it was over. No matter. Free at last!

I'm sure you also experienced the little frisson when *finally* after nine-tenths of the way into a whaling book we first hear (or read) the words "There she blows!" And from there, of course, the final 30 pages are a wild roller coaster ride to the ending with Ishmael, the Pequod's only survivor, bobbing on the open sea on Queequeg's coffin. And I'll bet you agree that the last tenth of the book really did roll along quite nicely (despite the unattributed quotes which drove me a bit nuts.)

But take a moment to deconstruct that phrase – "There (sometimes "Thar") she blows." Why "she?" I know all ships are female; but surely whales, who actually are male or female biologically, should have the right to be identified correctly. You protest, saying that at the distance of a mile there's no way of knowing the sex. True, but usually in grammatical situations in which the sex is undetermined, the masculine is used, right? Or at least it has always been thus until feminists took exception to this grammatical convenience and started demanding the cumbersome "he or she"s or "his or her"s that have become the hallmarks of PC prose from the 1970s on. Could it be that the women's libbers had already been able to make initial inroads in the early 1800s in the whaling community? Seems unlikely, doesn't it.

I might also add at this point that my last paragraph has given me serious second thoughts about how interesting this correspondence would be to anyone other than you and me. In fact, how interesting is it to *you*?

I've been putting this next realization off for as long as possible, but now it must be said: I am older than Ahab was when he was finally carried away by Moby Dick. The math is right there on the page. He was 18 when he went to sea for the first time and this voyage is 40 years later, making him 58. I – in case you haven't heard it on the news – am now 60!

The truth is I feel pretty chipper and I'm always confident that I can do my fast two and a half mile walk every morning because, after all, I just did it yesterday. I mean barring being hit by a car, having a heart attack or having my leg eaten by a white whale, one simply cannot deteriorate that much overnight, right? The trick, of course, is that I have to have done the walk yesterday. Ahab: "Starbuck, I am old;– shake hands with me."

This is all by way of invitation: do you want to go on the fast walk with me on Friday morning in Halifax, Nova Scotia, when we will be in that sea-faring city together?

Chapter 122 is my favorite in the whole book. And not just because it's a remarkably brief 36 words long. But because 9 of those words are "um;" 4 of them are "thunder;" and 2 of them are "rum." This means that 42% of the words in the entire chapter alliterate with each other. And you say the man was no poet.

You've probably noted in Melville's bio that he got fed up with fiction a few years after *Moby Dick* and dedicated himself to poetry. Do you think it was as good as Chapter 122? Doubtful.

Since you've read my play, you will be aware that I've been spending some time recently trying to understand Hamlet. So I was pleased to find a Hamlet moment in Starbuck's indecision about whether to shoot Ahab or not. There's Starbuck, the man with a conscience, knowing full well that Ahab is leading the crew to its death, and yet he is incapable of pulling the trigger on Ahab.

The scene is so strikingly similar to a moment in Hamlet in which the Prince is unable to rouse himself to killing Claudius while the King is praying that I'm sure Melville must have had Shakespeare's scene in mind as he wrote his own. In both scenes the potential victim is unaware of the presence of his would-be assassin – Claudius because he is praying; Ahab because he is sleeping. And in both instances the righteous assassin is unable to get the job done. Hamlet, of course, gets – and makes good on – another opportunity, Starbuck does not.

Why?

Because, as Ahab says, "Starbuck is Stubb reversed, and Stubb is Starbuck; and ye two are all mankind." This is not a book about men, about mere mortals and their quotidian affairs. This is a book about a man so overwhelmingly obsessed that he resembles those famously unprincipled and undeterred Greek gods. Men will do what men will do, but this game is played on a higher level.

Bringing me to Ahab. Throughout the book I have been harboring negative feelings about the man. And yet, despite his weirdness and all his negative obsessiveness, in the last fifty pages or so of the book I came to rather admire him. I mean the guy must have had something, some charisma or magnetism, to get the crew behind him in the first place. Then, even as he gets stranger and stranger (by the end, his best friend is Pip!), he continues by the sheer force of his personality to hold the crew in line.

(I mean imagine after the first two days' disastrous encounters with *Moby Dick* saying: Yeah, I think it's a good idea to go after him again – third time's a charm.)

I think it shows how much people want a strong leader to follow, even as wrong-headed and even mad as he may be. It's sort of like the existentialists' emphasis on passionate commitment. That commitment is a man becoming his true self they say. And I think it's something men do long for – to be passionately committed to some great enterprise. And when suddenly someone comes along and says: "Follow me to greatness!" men want to believe it. Witness Germany under Hitler. It's perhaps no accident that pre-existentialist Heidegger became the Nazi house intellectual.

And there's also my admiration for Ahab anticipating Dylan Thomas and not going gentle into that good night. Rage he certainly did. Of course it's inevitable that the light dies anyway in the end. But still – rage! Did you share any of this feeling of admiration for Ahab at the end? Of course, you're not yet 60.

terry.

25 August 2004 – Phoenix, but bound for Halifax

Terry.

No I did not admire Ahab. But I understand your admiration. I think I admired Queequeg, maybe not in the same way that the Governor of New Jersey would have admired him, but because he was the most natural. He seemed to have the least to prove. I love and admire people who have nothing to prove. Who just enjoy the moment.

[Just a couple of weeks prior to Steve's letter, the Governor of New Jersey, James McGreevey stunned the state by announcing he would resign his office. In his resignation speech he announced that he was a homosexual. TNH.]

I would not describe Melville as a guy who enjoyed the moment. No, he had way too much to prove. His only character who had nothing to prove was, in my opinion, Queequeg, which is why Melville had to make him a primitive and a savage. Because the heart of Melville's darkness was precisely that: he did not believe a very smart and knowledgeable man could ever be happy in a primitive, savage way. Melville believed that such a smart man would always be tormented by the hypocrisy of religious people, the imperfection of society's contracts, etc. Only a savage could relate to life on a truly day-to-day, indeed moment-to-moment basis. This tormented Melville to the point that it didn't matter to him if he passed his torment on to his readers.

Melville did prove one thing: put all of your conflicted inner selves into a novel, give them separate names, and let them fight it out and you'll sell 3,000 copies, max, in your own lifetime. Give me a robust Tom Wolfe novel any day. Give me a truly poetic writer writing for pure entertainment value.

I think your play, Terry, is at the level of Woody Allen's best work, and I believe it is because it shares its gifts with the reader and the audience (something Melville was too angry to consider, the-reader-be-damned is an attitude felt throughout his book, note: the unattributed quotes, etc.) and it is written to entertain. Tolstoy did the same thing and so did Shakespeare – Melville did not. I believe that the best artists are also the best entertainers. I don't think they are the same thing, but I do think that when you're on a roll, and you take the time to edit artistically, you can do both.

[On a "level of Woody Allen's best work"?! Steve has always been more than generous in his praise of my writing. And who's to say he's not right, that's what I say. His comments have brightened my days more times than I can count. Perhaps the reason I am so chuffed by his good opinion is that Steve is easily the cleverest, most creative person I've ever known. I say that with some basis for comparison since I spent my professional career working with creative people in advertising. Is this mutual admiration stuff making anyone ill yet? Okay, I'll stop. My only defense is that it's truly felt. TNH.]

steve.

5 September 2004 – Halifax, Nova Scotia.

Steve.

As I write this you are winging your way back to Arizona. Miranda and I will be on our Halifax-to-Toronto flight this evening, but while I had a few moments I did want to say how much I appreciated you and Kathy flying across the continent to be at Andrew's wedding here.

It was great to see you both. I wished we lived closer to each other and could get together more often. On the other hand, as Miranda points out, if we saw each other all the time, what a loss to literature. We would not have had the motivation to create this quirky minor classic of the age.

Frankly, I'd be willing to trade this immortality for the chance to sit and watch a few ballgames with you. Immortality is for the dead. (I trust that's suitably paradoxical.) Friendship is for the living.

I must say I loved our efforts here in Halifax to bring symbolic closure to our *Moby Dick* experience: the singing of whaling (or at least Maritime) songs at the Lower Deck pub. And, of course, the failed whale-sighting cruise we took. Well, what the hell, at least we got to see the Halifax harbour (note the appropriate Canadian spelling). Thinking about it afterwards it struck me that even in *Moby Dick* there are days and weeks that go by without the sighting of a *whale*, much less a great white one. So what made us think we'd be about to shout "Thar she blows!" on our brief two and a half hour cruise?

t.

[On our way to Canada at the end of August, Miranda and I had made a stop at the most beautiful of American racetracks in Saratoga Springs, New York. At the races I noted a horse called Steve's Thunder and on a hunch put two dollars on him to win. He didn't. I did, however, mention this to Steve and even gave him the losing ticket when we were in Halifax together. I'm telling you this, admittedly not very interesting, story because Steve's final Moby

Dick e-mail begins with an alternate version of the lyrics to Carly Simon's song "You're So Vain." TNH.]

8 September 2004 – Phoenix

Well, I hear you went up to Saratoga
And your horse (naturally won)   **(failed to win)**
Then you flew your Lear jet up to Nova Scotia
To see the (total eclipse of the sun)   **(whales but there was nary a fin)**

(alternative lyrics in bold)

Terry,

Just when I believe *Moby Dick* has become irrelevant, this quote jumps out at me from Tina Brown in today's *Washington Post*, "How long will it be till the news in Iraq gets so bad that even the most inattentive member of the voting public will start to wonder if our war president is not Winston Churchill, but Captain Ahab?"

So it was a great postscript to our writing this book together to be in Halifax for your son's wedding and the fruitless voyage we took on a tourist boat to attempt a whale-sighting. But somehow the beauty of the water and the whale's defiant absence from our view was fitting. I did get a sense of what Ishmael said about going to sea whenever he had just about had enough of foolish, land-locked mankind. As a way to refresh.

John Kennedy once remarked that we love the sea because we all come from the sea. A curiously evolutionary observation from a reputed lifelong Catholic. Maybe the Garden of Eden was under the sea. Maybe Eve was a mermaid and the serpent was a precursor to the Loch Ness monster. Jung wanted us to see how myths could be interchangeable, almost as interchangeable as players on baseball teams today.

(Today's baseball is getting closer and closer to sandlot ball where you choose up sides before each game, and today's teammate was yesterday's opponent. Melville would love such unresolved chaos. So baseball, like Melville, is badly in need of an editor. And now that we're done, perhaps we are too.)

steve.